nadiya's fast flavours

NADIYA'S FAST FLAVOURS

—

nadiya hussain

photography by chris terry
illustrations by léa maupetit

michael joseph
an imprint of
penguin books

This book is for the most chilled guy I know.
Who likes to do everything . . . nice . . . and . . . slow . . .
The only thing he does do fast, is eat.
Dawud

contents

introduction

The word 'fast' can take on many meanings. When I think of fast, I think about the long, hot, bubble-bath I dreamt about at midday and the speedy, tepid wash I had in comparison.

When I think of fast, I think of the mayhem of trying to get to a 9 a.m. appointment when it is 8:55, and you have barely cleared the house of children and packed lunches, knowing full well it takes you nine minutes to get there!

Fast to me is thinking I can clear out my cupboards in the gap between meetings; where I imagine I can decant and alphabetize all the contents of my overflowing shelves. You and I both know that has never happened, and once you have started you have just given yourself a week's worth of work that you did not need.

Fast can mean much more than the pace at which we live or at least attempt to live. I have fully accepted that life will happen at the speed it wants to, and I have no control over that. Yes, sometimes I think I have control, but if my life over the last few years is anything to go by, I just don't.

But what I can take full ownership and control over is the food I cook in my kitchen, from the meals cooked in vats for extended family, the weekly din-dins for my kids, the banana bread made between meetings or the pastry dough proving for croissants the following day. That is what I know I can control – and so can you. So, together let us take ownership of our creativity in the food we cook, and serve up some fast flavours.

The recipes in this book are all either fast in speed, or fast in flavour (and some of them are both!). By this I mean that there are recipes in here that you can simply cook very quickly and which are measured by the time you spend in the kitchen, while other recipes are more about taking shortcuts, using tinned ingredients or getting clever with leftovers, giving you something flavoursome and delicious with comparatively less of a wait.

Thanks to such shortcuts, recipes like the One-Pan Cheese and Egg Sandwich, Lentil Hummus, Banana Skin Bagels, or Choco-Mint Roll all take up less time than they might, but are still crammed with all the deliciousness!

My Bombay Patty Burgers, Sumac Plums, Baked Beans Dirty Rice and Tamarind Chicken are recipes that you can pack full of flavour faster than you can click your fingers, all because of the ingredients you use, elevating them, making them a little bit more scrummy, crammed with all the flavour your heart desires!

So, as it's all about flavour, I have chaptered this book the best way I know how. You know those times when you are on your way home from a hard day's work and you start a sentence in your head or begin tapping out a text message or whisper involuntarily, 'I fancy something . . .'

Well, let me help you end that thought! Do you fancy something spicy? Something cheesy, perhaps? Maybe something fresh and zesty, or fragrant and herby? Or something unapologetically sweet? There are eight great chapters in this book – Herby, Spicy, Cheesy, Nutty, Zesty, Earthy, Fruity and Sweet – all written to help you end that sentence and find the recipe that satisfies that burning need for something . . . whatever that something might be.

In this book you will find your something and I can guarantee it will be packed with flavour, whether it is fast and delicious, or full of delicious flavour hacks. It's yours to devour. So, devour the pages, the words, the recipes, the photos and go to town on creating great flavours.

HERBY

———

fish mousse dumpling soup

These light, herby dumplings are made with white fish blitzed into a simple mousse. They are dropped into a seasoned soup base where they gently poach, and are then drizzled with a vibrant herb dressing. This is fresh and easy. Easy to make, easy to eat.

For the dumplings

2 fresh jalapeños, sliced

a handful of fresh dill (15g)

a handful of fresh chives (15g)

3 cloves of garlic

2 haddock fillets, chopped into chunks (260g)

½ teaspoon salt

1 egg

4 tablespoons plain flour

For the soup base

1.5 litres hot water

4 fish stock cubes

1 tablespoon fish sauce

1 tablespoon soy sauce

For the herb dressing

50ml olive oil

juice of 1 lime

1 tablespoon mayonnaise

Start by adding the jalapeños, dill, chives and garlic to a food processor. Blitz to a fine mixture and then remove 2 tablespoons' worth out into a jam jar.

Add the fish pieces, salt, egg and flour to the food processor and whizz to a smooth paste. If the mixture looks loose, add another spoonful of flour and mix till you have a consistency that can be picked up and shaped.

To make the soup base, put the hot water, stock cubes, fish sauce and soy sauce in a large pan, bring to a boil and, as soon as it does, turn it right down.

Take a heaped tablespoon at a time of the fish mousse paste and, using oiled hands, shape into balls and add gently to the broth. You should have eight to ten good-size dumplings. Leave them to sit in the simmering water, uncovered, for 10 minutes.

Make the dressing by putting the olive oil and lime juice in the jam jar with the herbs. Add the mayo and give it a good shake.

Serve each bowl of soup with 2–3 dumplings and a drizzle of the herb dressing.

serves 4   prep 25 mins   cook 15 mins

cheese and chive cullen skink

This is my take on a cullen skink, which to me has always seemed like a fuss-free one-pot fish pie. It is rich, creamy and flavoured with chives, and I like to add sweet potatoes for colour and sweetness. To finish, a crumbly sprinkling of salty, spiced, crispy cheese and some finely chopped chives.

30g unsalted butter

6 anchovy fillets

170g tin of crab meat (120g drained weight)

2 large leeks, washed and thinly sliced

½ teaspoon salt

2 tablespoons plain flour

300g sweet potatoes, peeled and cut into mouth-size chunks

750ml fish stock

400g fish pie mix

150ml double cream

30g fresh chives, finely chopped

For the topping
150g Cheddar cheese, finely grated

a sprinkle of paprika

a handful of finely chopped chives

Start by melting the butter in a medium saucepan. As soon as the butter has melted, add the anchovy fillets and mix. Add the drained crab meat and cook until crisp and golden. Throw in the leek and salt and cook for about 10 minutes till the leek is soft. As soon as it is, add the flour and mix through for a minute to cook the flour out.

Add the sweet potato and the fish stock, bring to the boil and turn down as soon as it does. Simmer for 10 minutes, till the potato is just cooked.

Preheat the oven to 200°C/fan 180°C and line a baking tray.

Add the fish and stir through, then cook gently on a medium heat for 10–12 minutes. You will know the fish is cooked when the flesh feels firmer and is no longer translucent. When that happens, add the cream and chives, stir through and leave to simmer with the lid on for 5 minutes.

To make the topping, layer the cheese onto the baking tray, pop into the oven and watch and wait for the cheese to melt and become golden all over and crisp. This takes about 10 minutes but you need to keep checking and turning the tray in the oven so that it cooks evenly. As soon as it does, take out, sprinkle with paprika and leave to cool and crisp up some more. Take the cheese and crumble into a cheesy dust in your hands.

Serve up the hot cullen skink with a sprinkling of the cheese topping and some finely chopped chives.

serves 4

prep 25 mins

cook 45 mins

herb fritters with lemony yoghurt

These herb fritters are the way I use up bags of wilting salad and sad herbs on their way out. The leaves are simply blitzed and mixed with five spice, onion and egg, then cooked into small fritters of green goodness. I like to serve them with this lemony yoghurt dressing.

For the fritters

2 onions

100g bag of green salad leaves (rocket or a mix)

30g parsley

1 teaspoon panch puran (Indian five-spice)

1 teaspoon salt

4 tablespoons chickpea flour

3 medium eggs

oil for frying

For the lemon yoghurt dressing

200g Greek yoghurt

50ml whole milk

1 lemon, zest only

a pinch of salt

2 teaspoons chilli flakes

Very thinly slice the onions and pop into a bowl (you need to slice them very thinly so they cook fast).

Add the salad leaves to a food processor with the parsley and five-spice and blend till you have something that is well mixed and not chunky. It should look a bit like finely chopped herbs. Add the mixture to the onion with the salt and mix. Add the chickpea flour and mix in till combined. Add the eggs and mix through.

Pop a large non-stick frying pan onto the heat and pour in enough oil to cover the base of the pan. Heat to a high heat.

Take tablespoons of the mixture and drop gently into the pan – you will have to do these in a few batches. Fry for 1½ minutes on each side, then put onto a plate lined with kitchen paper.

Once you have fried them all, make the dressing by adding the yoghurt and milk to a bowl with the lemon zest and salt. Mix.

Arrange the fritters on a platter and drizzle over the yoghurt dressing.

Heat any oil remaining in the pan (if there is not any, add 2 tablespoons). Sprinkle in the chilli flakes and as soon as they start to sizzle, dollop over the yoghurt and serve.

makes 20

prep 20 mins

cook 15 mins

potato pockets

This is the kind of recipe that can suit any mealtime, and it's a rival for all weekend breakfasts! Filled with soft herby mashed potato and an encased runny egg yolk, it's the layers of delicious flavour that make these crisp filo pastry pockets totally special.

400g mashed potato

3 cloves of garlic, minced

½ bunch of fresh dill (15g)

½ bunch of fresh parsley (15g)

1 teaspoon celery (or fine) salt

11 sheets of filo pastry

7 eggs, separated

1 tablespoon cornflour

1 tablespoon paprika

½ teaspoon salt

oil, for frying

Sriracha, to serve (optional)

Decant the mash into a bowl and mash till smoother. Add the minced garlic to the mash.

Chop the dill and parsley, as fine as you can get it, and add to the potato. Add the celery salt and mix. Set aside.

Take the filo rectangles and cut in half, so you now have 22 sheets of filo. Lay out 7 sheets of filo side by side, brush with egg white and top each sheet with another sheet of filo.

Divide the mash mixture equally onto the 7 sheets, placing the herby mash in the centre. Using the back of a spoon, create a dent where your egg yolks will sit. All yolks are different sizes, so you make the dent based on the yolks you have. Use your spoon to square off the mash around the edges. Do this to all 7 and drop an egg yolk into each dent.

Brush the excess filo around the edge of the potato with the egg white. Add a filo square on top and be sure to seal the edges where you brushed all over with the egg whites. You will have one square left over, so just give one parcel a double lid. Extra crispy!

Brush the top of the parcel all over with the egg white. Take the top edge and fold down into the centre (you may need to tuck in the shorter sides first, then fold the longer side over the top). Take the bottom edge and fold up into the centre. Brush all over with egg white. Fold over the left side into the centre and then the right. Do this to all of them and pop onto a baking tray.

Take the egg whites and lightly whisk till foamy. Add the cornflour, paprika and salt and whisk till combined.

Pop a non-stick pan over a high heat with 1cm of oil.

makes
7
pockets

prep
30
mins

cook
10
mins

Dip one of the squares into the egg white mix and coat all over.
Place carefully into the oil, yolk side still up, and fry for 1½ minutes,
then flip over for 1 minute to brown before draining. Repeat this
with the others, and they are ready to serve, hopefully with a runny
yolk in the centre. I like to drizzle over a generous squirt of Sriracha.

spinach and coriander crepes

It's the secret layer of grated cheese and egg yolk and a sneaky spreading of piccalilli rolled up inside that put these fresh green crepes into a league all of their own. Proof that simple can still be delicious!

For the crepes

5 large egg whites

a small handful of spinach (30g)

a large handful of fresh coriander

1 teaspoon black pepper

1 teaspoon salt

1 teaspoon ground cumin

80g plain flour

200ml water

2 tablespoons oil

oil, for frying

For the filling

5 large egg yolks

25g Cheddar cheese, finely grated

150g piccalilli, chopped

Start by adding the egg whites, spinach, coriander, pepper, salt and cumin to a food processor and blitz.

Put the mixture in a bowl, add the flour, water and oil and whisk till you have a runny crepe batter, the same consistency as double cream. You can do all of this in a food processor to save some time. Leave to sit for 5 minutes.

Mix the yolks with the cheese in a small bowl.

Pop a pancake pan or small non-stick pan onto a high heat and brush with oil. Add just less than a ladleful of the crepe mixture into the centre and swirl the pan around so the base is covered with a thin sheet of the crepe.

As soon as the top looks dry, brush on the egg and cheese mixture and leave on the heat for 30 seconds to warm the egg through and just melt the cheese. Then spread over the piccalilli and roll. Do this till you have made them all.

makes 8 crepes   prep 15 mins   cook 15 mins

rosemary rump dinner

I love cooking with rump because it's a cheap cut of meat that goes a long way, especially alongside veg. This recipe uses a ready-to-go soffritto (a basic mix of diced onions, carrots, celery, etc, available frozen from supermarkets), not just as a base but for the veg itself, cooked into a stew with rosemary, ginger and mustard. The stew is served topped with the sliced rump and drizzled with an infused oil.

For the stew

3 tablespoons oil

1 large sprig of fresh rosemary, stalks removed

500g frozen soffritto mix (veg base mix as it is often otherwise known)

1 teaspoon salt

1 lime, zest and juice

2 tablespoons ginger paste

2 tablespoons Dijon mustard

1 tablespoon tomato paste

2 tablespoons cornflour

1 litre chicken or lamb stock

100g basmati rice

For the rump

2 x 400g lamb rumps

salt, for sprinkling

For the oil

1 small sprig of fresh rosemary, leaves removed and roughly chopped

100ml olive oil

1 lime, zest and juice

Preheat the oven to the highest you can get it (mine gets to 250°C/fan 230°C).

Align the rumps on a baking tray. Sprinkle generously with salt. Put the rump into the oven and leave to cook till the outside of the flesh is completely dark – this should take 20 minutes (it doesn't need turning). As soon as it's dark, turn the oven off and leave the rump in there for the duration of the cook.

Now, to make the stew start by adding the oil to a casserole dish along with the rosemary. As soon as the oil is hot and the rosemary is sizzling, add the soffritto, mix in and cook till golden brown and soft – this should take 10 minutes. Add the salt, juice and zest of the lime and throw the whole lime in – we can get rid of it later.

Add the ginger, mustard and tomato and cook for a few minutes. Add the cornflour and mix through till the flour is coated. Add the stock and rice. Take out the lime and leave to simmer away for 30 minutes until thickened and reduced.

Once the oven has cooled down to the touch but is still warm, take out the rump. Turn off the stew.

Make the dressing by mixing in a jar the rosemary, oil, salt, lime juice and zest. Shake well.

Slice up the rump, serve on top of the stew and drizzle on some of that oil to finish.

serves 4

prep 20 mins

cook 1 hour

salsa verde side of salmon

This is a wonderful centre-of-the-table type of dish, a whole side of salmon baked with a punchy salsa verde. It's served with onion wedges cooked gently in a medley of simple flavoursome miso and ghee, and the crispy salmon skin crumbled on top. Nothing wasted, everything used, and stunning to look at and eat.

For the onions

6 onions, peeled and halved, intact at the root

2 tablespoons ghee, melted

3 tablespoons miso paste

½ teaspoon salt

For the crispy skin

1.5kg side of salmon, scaled and pin-boned (ask your fishmonger to separate the salmon and skin but keep the skin)

2 tablespoons cornflour

1 tablespoon paprika

½ teaspoon salt

For the salsa verde

100g ghee (it doesn't need to be melted as it will be whizzed together in the food processor)

2 tablespoons balsamic vinegar

95g tin of sardines, in oil

40g capers

3 cloves of garlic

½ teaspoon salt

2 x 30g packs of fresh parsley

100g panko breadcrumbs

Start by preheating the oven to 200°C/fan 180°C. Have a roasting dish big enough to lay the salmon in comfortably and another flat tray to lay the skin. Line both with baking paper.

Add the onions to the roasting dish, drizzle over the ghee, add the miso paste and salt and get your hands in there to give it a good mix. Lay the onions flat-side down.

Pat the skin dry and cut the salmon in half. In a bowl, mix the cornflour, paprika and salt. Coat the cornflour mix over the skin until it is coated all over. Lay flat on the prepared baking tray.

Pop the onions in the oven on the middle shelf and the skin just below. Leave in for 20 minutes while you prep the salsa. Make sure to flip the skin over halfway through cooking so it crisps up evenly.

Put the ghee, vinegar, sardines and their oil, capers, garlic, salt, parsley and breadcrumbs into a food processor and whizz till well combined.

Take out the tray with the onions, move the onions over to the sides and place the salmon in the centre. Take the salsa verde and spread it over until all the salmon top is covered.

Bake in the oven for another 30–35 minutes. After 20 minutes, take the crispy skin out and leave to cool.

As soon as the salmon is ready, serve it on a platter with the onions. Crumble the crispy skin all over and it is ready to eat.

recipe photographs over page ▶

serves 6–8

prep 30 mins

cook 55 mins

tarragon chicken

Tarragon is a herb I never ate or used until very recently, when I finally realised how good it is with chicken and garlic and, ooooooh, cream, all the cream! Served with broccoli and tagliatelle, this is my all-in-one-pan chicken dinner of tarragon dreams.

85g unsalted butter

5 cloves of garlic, thinly sliced

1 large broccoli head, broken into small florets, stem trimmed and grated

1 teaspoon salt

8 boneless, skinless chicken thighs, slashed but not cut all the way through

1 teaspoon yeast extract

a large handful of fresh tarragon

300g tagliatelle

125ml cream

1 lemon, for squeezing

freshly ground black pepper, to serve

Start by adding the butter to a large, flat casserole dish. Bring to the heat and allow the butter to melt until it starts sizzling. Keep heating the butter till it begins to just brown. Add the garlic straight away in an even layer and let it just become golden.

As soon as it does, add the grated broccoli stem and cook till the stem has really softened and almost melted down (this will take about 8 minutes).

Season with the salt and mix, then add the chicken pieces along with the yeast extract. Cover and leave to simmer for 15–20 minutes.

Meanwhile, put the pasta on to cook, following the instructions on the packet.

Once the chicken is nearly cooked through, halve the broccoli florets and add to the chicken. Cover, lower the heat and allow to steam for 5 minutes. Add the tarragon and mix through.

Drain the pasta, reserving some of that starchy water. Add the pasta to the chicken and mix through. Add a ladle of the starch water and simmer, uncovered, to allow the liquid to cook out.

Add the cream, mix and leave for a few minutes for the cream to thicken and it is ready to serve, with a squeeze of lemon and some freshly ground black pepper, if you like.

serves 4 · prep 15 mins · cook 40 mins

banana thyme loaf

We all love a banana bread. But when you can't decide between baking a favourite, or baking something a little bit different, this is the perfect compromise: a moist banana bread flavoured with the aroma of thyme and finished off with a sticky sweet salted caramel.

4 small bananas, 3 mashed (340g prepped weight), 1 sliced lengthways

50g salted butter, melted, plus extra for greasing the tin

175g caster sugar

a pinch of salt

a large sprig of fresh thyme, leaves picked

120ml olive oil

75ml whole milk, at room temperature

300g self-raising flour, sifted

For the salted caramel

100g caster sugar

45g salted butter

60ml cream

½ teaspoon salt flakes

Put the mashed bananas in a bowl and leave out for half an hour to oxidize – this will make them browner and add to the colour. Or if you are in a rush, just mash the bananas and get to baking the loaf.

Line and grease a 900g loaf tin and preheat the oven to 180°C/fan 160°C.

Add the butter and caster sugar to the banana and mix till combined, then add the salt and thyme leaves, reserving a few to sprinkle over at the end. Now pour in the olive oil and milk and mix through. Add the sifted flour and fold through until you have a smooth cake batter.

Pour the mixture into the tin and level off with a few sharp taps, add the two slices of banana, cut-side up, and bake for 50 minutes–1 hour, covering loosely for the last 15 minutes to stop the top browning too much. You will know the cake is ready when a skewer inserted comes out clean.

Meanwhile, make the caramel by adding the sugar in an even layer into the base of a pan, on medium to low heat, and watch as the sugar turns to caramel, stirring it occasionally. As soon as the sugar melts, add the butter. If you find it seizing, don't worry, just keep stirring over a very low heat and the caramel will come together. As soon as the butter has melted, add the cream. Cook on a low heat for 2 minutes till you have smooth caramel. Take off the heat.

Remove the cake from the oven and leave to cool in the tin for 10 minutes, then take out and leave to cool on a wire rack.

As soon as it has cooled enough, drizzle over the caramel. If you find it has become too stiff, warm through gently and then drizzle. You will have caramel left over but not to worry, because we all need a little extra caramel and it's perfect served on the side for anyone who wants some more to pour over. Sprinkle with a few thyme leaves, if you like.

serves 8–10

prep 25 mins

cook 1 hour

choco-mint roll

This is one of my favourite no-bake bakes, which is why we can justify spending a little time on the minty decorations. The roll can be made with either leftover or shop-bought cake, broken up, flattened, filled and rolled with so much minty goodness. Top with chocolate-coated mint leaves – it's fresh, fresh, fresh!

For the decoration
about 35 large fresh mint leaves

60g dark chocolate

For the cake
20 chocolate-covered mini rolls (2 packs)

For the mint ganache
50g milk chocolate, chopped

50ml double cream

¼ teaspoon mint extract

For the mint cream
150ml double cream

1½ tablespoons caster sugar

10 fresh mint leaves

Start by lining a baking tray with paper and laying about 35 mint leaves of varying sizes on it, with their undersides facing upwards. Heat the chocolate till just starting to melt and mix until it is runny. Brush the underside of the leaves with chocolate and leave to set, chocolate-side down. Once they are all done, pop in the fridge.

Now line a 23cm square cake tin and set aside.

Take the mini rolls out of the packets and add to a food processor. Blitz till the mixture begins to form a dough. Drop into the lined tin and use the back of a spoon to flatten into a neat, flat, tight layer. Leave in the fridge while you get on to the rest.

Make the ganache by putting the chocolate and cream into a pan. Pop onto a low heat and leave to melt, stirring occasionally. As soon as the chocolate has melted, mix in the mint extract and bring the mixture together to a smooth, even, glossy ganache. Put aside to leave to cool.

To make the mint cream, put the cream in a bowl. Add the sugar and mint leaves to a mortar and use your pestle to grind to a minty green wet sugar. Start whipping the cream and as soon as it begins to thicken, add the sugar and mix through. Take the cake out of the tin and layer the cream evenly on top.

Roll the cake, starting with the edge closest to you and using the paper underneath to help. As soon as you get to the end, place seam-side down and pop into the fridge to firm up for half an hour. If the roll cracks, just pinch to bring together. As bakes go, it's forgiving, so go for it.

As soon as the roll is out of the fridge, spread a thin layer of ganache over it, then stick your minty leaves on to it to decorate.

serves 8

prep 25 mins + chilling

cook 10 mins

lemon basil shortbread

These buttery shortbread biscuits are just joyous. They are flavoured with fresh basil and filled with jam and white chocolate. If you can resist eating them all by yourself (which is not easy!), they make great presents, tumbled into a jar and tied with a ribbon.

50g unsalted butter, softened

110g caster sugar, plus extra for dusting

15 fresh basil leaves, finely chopped

1 lemon, zest only

1 teaspoon vanilla bean paste

400g plain flour, plus extra for dusting

For sandwiching

4 tablespoons raspberry jam

50g white chocolate, grated

Mix the butter and sugar till light and fluffy. Add the chopped basil, lemon zest and vanilla and mix to incorporate well. Add the flour and mix till you form a dough. Be sure not to knead, simply bring together.

Flatten into a round, wrap in cling film and leave to chill in the fridge for at least half an hour. Have four baking trays lined with some baking paper ready.

Take out the dough, dust the surface with flour and roll the dough out into a sheet about 3mm thin. Using a 6cm round cutter, cut out rounds and place on the trays with a gap of 1cm between them. Keep cutting, bringing together the excess and re-rolling till you have 48 biscuits, or have used up all the dough.

Prick the surface of each biscuit twice using a fork and pop the trays into the fridge for 30 minutes. Preheat the oven to 180°C/ fan 160°C.

Take the trays out of the fridge and generously sprinkle each one with sugar. Bake in the oven for 10–12 minutes, till lightly golden. Take out and leave to cool completely on the tray before removing.

Mix the jam and the white chocolate. Dollop some jam on the underside of a biscuit and top with another biscuit. Do this to all the biscuits. Once you have made all your biscuits, enjoy and store in an airtight container if there are any left, if being the operative word!

makes
24

prep
25 mins
+ chilling

cook
each batch for 10 mins

honey sage cake

This cake is as beautiful as it is delicious, baked with whole sage leaves arranged on the top and around the edge. The sponge is sweet and rich from muscovado sugar and blossom honey, and the sage flavour is a welcome change. Sage is not just for onion, or for stuffing, now it's for cake too!

For the cake

170g blossom honey (or any honey you have)

140g unsalted butter, plus extra for greasing

85g light muscovado sugar

10 fresh sage leaves, chopped, plus plenty extra for lining the tin

2 medium eggs

1 orange, zest only (reserve the juice)

200g self-raising flour, sifted

For the honey icing

55g icing sugar, sifted

1 tablespoon honey

1 tablespoon hot water

Start by adding the honey, butter, muscovado and chopped sage leaves into a pan and heating till the sugar has dissolved. Take off the heat and leave to cool completely.

Grease a round 18cm cake tin, base and sides, and line the base with paper. Preheat the oven to 180°C/fan 160°C. Add whole sage leaves around the inside edges of the cake tin and some nicely arranged in the base.

Once the butter mixture has cooled, pour into a bowl and add the eggs and orange zest. Whisk for a few minutes till light and fluffy (this should take no more than 2 minutes). Add the flour and fold through till you have a smooth batter.

Pour into the prepared cake tin and bake for 40–45 minutes until a skewer inserted into the middle of the cake comes out clean. As soon as the cake is baked and while still hot, pour over the orange juice and leave to soak. Leave in the tin to cool.

Make the icing by mixing together the icing sugar, honey and water. Take the cake out, turn sage-side up and spread over the icing.

makes 8–10 prep 20 mins cook 45 mins

SPICY

ginger, pear and oat pudding

We love overnight oats in our house because they take the stress out of the morning rush. Sometimes, though, I forget to make them the night before, but when I've promised something, I like to deliver. So this is my fast version: speedy oats with no need to sit overnight, made quicker by blending the oats down to a fine powder so that the liquid gets soaked up faster. This is flavoured with ground ginger and grated pear, as we all know ginger loves pear and pear loves ginger.

100g pecans

200g oats

100g raisins

1 teaspoon ground ginger

4 small pears, skin on, grated

400ml coconut water

4 tablespoons runny honey

To serve

160ml coconut cream

honey

nut butter

Toast the pecans in a dry pan till they've darkened in colour – this should only take a few minutes so be careful they don't burn. Pop into a bowl and leave to cool. In the same pan, toast the oats until they are an even golden brown. Add to the bowl with the pecans and leave to cool.

Add the oats and pecans to a food processor and whizz till fine.

Put the mixture into a bowl, along with the raisins and ground ginger, and mix.

Add half the grated pear along with the coconut water and honey and mix. Leave the mixture in the fridge for 20 minutes to soak up all the liquid.

To serve, add a dollop of the coconut cream on top, a dollop of the nut butter, and then sprinkle some more grated pear and a drizzle of honey.

serves
4

prep
10 mins

cook
30 mins

masala on-the-go buns

These are as fun as they are delicious. The buns are hollowed, filled with a masala egg mix, and baked. What could be simpler or more satisfying? They are great to eat as soon as they are baked or can be wrapped for on-the-go enjoyment.

1 small red onion, very finely chopped

½ teaspoon salt

6 unsliced burger buns

ketchup/brown sauce, for squirting

1 teaspoon dried chilli flakes

1 teaspoon cumin seeds, smashed

4 medium eggs

30g Cheddar cheese, finely grated

Start by finely dicing the onion and putting in a bowl with the salt. Using your hands, macerate the onions and leave to soften for 10 minutes.

Take the buns and if they are joined together, tear them apart straight down the middle so they are in two lines of three.

Now, using a knife, create a cavity in all six of the buns from the outside edge and stand them upright, side by side, in a 900g loaf tin so the hole side is exposed.

Squirt a little ketchup or brown sauce into each hole.

Add the chilli flakes and cumin seeds to the softened onion and mix. Add the eggs and whisk with a fork. Mix in the cheese and pour the mixture into a jug with a spout to make for easy pouring.

Preheat the oven to 180°C/fan 160°C.

Pour the mixture into the holes till you have filled up all six.

Bake in the oven for 15 minutes. Take out and leave in the tin for 5 minutes. Pull the buns apart and eat.

recipe photographs over page ▶

serves 6   prep 15 mins   cook 15 mins

panzanella salad

Panzanella salad is often made using stale leftover bread. No such thing in my house. So, I am making this because I love bread and that is okay. I've added a little difference with spices, toasted up and infused in a fragrant oil, so when it soaks into the bread it imparts all its flavour.

1 small French baguette, chopped or torn into 1cm pieces

150ml extra-virgin olive oil, plus more for drizzling

1 teaspoon mustard seeds

1 teaspoon dried chilli flakes

3 cloves of garlic, minced

1 red onion, diced

1 yellow pepper, diced

1 red pepper, diced

a pinch of salt, plus extra

10 cherry tomatoes, halved

100g black olives, pitted, halved

4 tablespoons balsamic vinegar

2 tablespoons English mustard

a handful of roughly chopped fresh parsley

Start by putting the bread in a large bowl.

Pour the oil into a frying pan and heat on a high heat.

As soon as the oil is hot, add the mustard seeds and when they begin to pop, add the chilli flakes and the garlic, lower the heat and stir till the garlic has just browned.

Add the onion and peppers with a pinch of salt and cook till just soft.

Add the tomatoes and olives to the bowl with the bread and use your hands to just squash some of those tomatoes to release the juices. Season with some more salt. Drizzle the oil mixture over them and mix in.

Mix the balsamic vinegar and mustard together. Drizzle all over the salad and mix in with the parsley. This is delicious eaten straight away, but equally as delicious when left for the bread to really absorb the flavours, so that is up to you. I personally cannot resist and have to go straight in.

serves
4

prep
10 mins

cook
15–20 mins

Turkish eggs

I discovered these eggs on my travels and found myself eating plate after plate after plate. So, I've made my version, with blended sweetcorn mixed in with the yoghurt for a twist, then topped with a poached egg and drizzled with a garlic chilli oil.

For the corn yoghurt

340g tin of sweetcorn

200g yoghurt

½ lemon, zest and juice

a pinch of salt

For the garlic chilli oil

100ml olive oil

1 garlic clove, sliced

2 teaspoons dried chilli flakes

To serve

4 eggs

salt and ground black pepper

fresh chopped chives

toast

Start by making the corn yoghurt. Drain the corn and squeeze till there is very little liquid left. Put in a food processer and blend with a tablespoon of the yoghurt. Transfer the mixture into a bowl with the rest of the yoghurt, lemon zest and juice and mix in with the salt.

To poach all the eggs at once, take a large saucepan of water and bring to the boil. As soon as it has boiled, reduce the heat. Take a spoon and remove any air bubbles in the base of the pot, being careful not to stir or swirl too much.

Crack the eggs into four small bowls or cups. Drop them into the water, one by one, as close to the water as possible. These should take 3–4 minutes, depending on the size of the eggs. Have a cold bowl of water ready on the side. Using a slotted spoon, remove the eggs and leave in cold water.

Divide the yoghurt mixture among four small plates. Place a poached egg in the centre of each.

Pour the oil into a small pan and heat on high. Add the garlic and cook till brown. Take off the heat, add the chilli flakes, salt and pepper and swirl.

Drizzle the garlic chilli oil over all of the four eggs, season with salt and pepper and sprinkle over the chives. Serve with toast.

serves 4

prep 15 mins

cook 10 mins

green chilli chops

This is my little boy's absolute ultimate fave. The chops are marinated in green chillies, pineapple and herbs, tenderized and then grilled to perfection. I have been modest in the weight of chops I have specified, but we have been known to hit the 4kg mark in our house! These are out of this world, but don't take it from me, make them and see.

220g tin of pineapple, drained

2 teaspoons ginger paste

2 teaspoons garlic paste

1 small onion, quartered

a large handful of fresh coriander

10 Thai green chillies

1 teaspoon ground turmeric

1 teaspoon garam masala

2 teaspoons coriander seeds

2 teaspoons salt

5 tablespoons oil, plus extra for griddling

900g lamb loin chops

To serve

yoghurt

pomegranate seeds

Start by making the marinade. Squeeze any moisture from the pineapple and put in a food processor. Add the ginger, garlic and onion and blend.

Add the coriander, chillies, turmeric, garam masala and coriander seeds. Now add the salt and oil and blend till you have a smooth mixture. If you find the mix is not moving, add a tablespoon of oil at a time till it moves.

Put the chops on a tray and pour the marinade all over. Get your hands in and cover the chops. Cover in cling film and leave overnight or for at least 4 hours in the fridge.

To cook, put a griddle on the hob on a high heat and brush generously with oil. Griddle the chops for a few minutes on each side, making sure to sear the fat on each chop.

Arrange on a platter, drizzle over yoghurt and sprinkle with pomegranate seeds for coolness.

recipe photographs over page ▶

serves
4–6

prep
41 mins
/2 hrs

cook
15 mins

carrot pepper pasta

Easy pasta recipes are a thing we all need to get on board with, whether you have kids, a large family, a tight budget or are incredibly time poor, or, like me, all of the above. In which case, this recipe is perfect. Made out of tinned carrots and flavoured to the nines, this simple sauce is stirred through with pasta, peas and prawns. It's bright and delicious, but most of all, quick!

300g dried pasta

100ml olive oil

3 cloves of garlic

2 tablespoons coriander seeds

400g tin of carrots, drained

1 teaspoon salt

2 teaspoons ground black pepper

2 tablespoons balsamic vinegar

200g frozen peas

300g cooked prawns

To serve
chopped fresh coriander

red chillies, sliced

Start by cooking the pasta according to the packet instructions.

Put the oil in a blender with the garlic. Lightly toast the coriander seeds in a dry pan till golden. Add to the garlic and blitz. Now add the drained carrots, salt, pepper and balsamic and whizz to a smooth mixture.

Just before the pasta has finished boiling, add the peas and allow to thaw out. Drain the pasta and add back into the pan. Pour over the sauce to warm through with the pasta.

Add the cooked prawns and stir through to heat.

To serve, sprinkle over the chopped coriander and chilli.

serves
4

prep
10 mins

cook
10–12 mins

beef cashew vindaloo

If you like spicy food then this is for you, with chilli in the sauce two ways, and more on top. It's balanced gently with aromatic spices and a drizzle of cashew cream, something my husband would normally laugh at because he can eat more spice than anyone I know, but even he loves the gentle tickle of the spices.

For the curry

4 tablespoons oil

100g cashews

1 teaspoon fennel seeds

1 cinnamon stick

3 bay leaves

5 cardamom pods

6 dried long chillies

4 onions, diced

4 tablespoons garlic paste

4 tablespoons ginger paste

1 tablespoon salt

6 tomatoes, diced

1 teaspoon ground turmeric

1 tablespoon chilli powder

2 teaspoons ground cumin

2 teaspoons curry powder

1kg diced beef

For the rice

400g basmati rice

a pinch of salt

2 black cardamom pods

To serve

100g cashews

a pinch of salt

green chillies

fresh coriander

3 spring onions

Make the curry first. Pour the oil into a large pan and as soon as the oil is hot, add the cashews and gently brown. Add the fennel, cinnamon, bay leaves, cardamom and chillies and warm through to release the flavours.

Add the onion and cook till very golden brown and dark. As soon as it is, add the garlic, ginger and salt and cook through. Add the tomatoes and cook till soft.

Now add the turmeric, chilli powder, cumin and curry powder and mix, cooking them till the oil rises to the surface. This indicates the spices have cooked through.

Add the beef, stir and cover with 500ml hot water. Leave to very gently simmer for 3 hours.

To make the rice, wash the rice till the water runs clear. Put in a large pan with 800ml cold water, the salt and cardamom pods. Stir, making sure the rice does not stick on the base. As soon as it comes to the boil, keep mixing till the water has really reduced. Lower the heat, cover and leave to steam with the lid on for 7 minutes.

Make the cashew cream by putting the cashews in a blender with the salt and just enough hot water to cover the cashews, then blend to a cream.

Once everything is ready, serve the rice with the vindaloo and a drizzle of cashew cream. Chop the chillies, coriander and spring onions and sprinkle on top.

serves
4–6

prep
10 mins

cook
3 hours

harissa chicken

Harissa is one of my favourite ingredients to cook with, especially like this where it's combined with chicken and the tang from preserved lemons, perfectly made to sit on a bed of smooth butter bean mash. This is bold and comforting.

8 boneless chicken thighs, skin on (575g)

4 tablespoons plain flour

1 teaspoon ground turmeric

1 teaspoon salt

6 tablespoons oil

4 red onions, quartered

½ teaspoon salt

90g harissa paste

3 preserved lemons, roughly chopped

300ml water

For the butter bean mash

6 tablespoons oil

3 cloves of garlic, minced

3 x 400g tins of butter beans, drained, reserving the juice

1 lemon, zest only

a pinch of salt

Put the thighs on a baking tray. Mix the flour, turmeric and salt in a bowl till combined and then use to coat the chicken completely.

Pour the oil into a large shallow pan and heat on medium. As soon as the oil is hot, add the chicken and fry till crisp and golden on both sides.

Take the chicken out and discard 3 tablespoons of the oil. Add the onion to the pan with some salt and cook till just starting to get soft.

Add the harissa and lemons and mix through. Add the chicken back in along with any juices, then pour in the water and leave to simmer.

Meanwhile, make the mash by pouring oil into another pan. As soon as the oil is hot, add the garlic and cook till brown. Add the beans and lemon zest and warm through, then use a masher to squash those beans down. If the mash is too dry, pour in a little of the juices from the chicken pan to loosen, stirring in until you reach the desired consistency. Season with salt.

The sauce should have thickened and the chicken is now ready to eat with the butter bean mash.

recipe photographs over page ▶

serves 4

prep 10 mins

cook 40–45 mins

cherry cinnamon dump cake

This does what it says on the tin: everything gets dumped. The cherries, the dry cake mix and then the melted butter all go in care-free, and then it's baked. What comes out has cakey bits, crunchy bits, oozy bits and gooey bits; it's the perfect imperfect cake for those of us who just need something sweet and need it now.

For the fruit
500g cherries, pitted and halved

70g caster sugar

1 teaspoon ground cinnamon

2 tablespoons cornflour

a pinch of salt

For the cake
200g caster sugar

150g plain flour

25g cocoa

1 teaspoon ground cinnamon

1 teaspoon baking powder

a pinch of salt

200g unsalted butter, melted

To serve
chocolate ice cream

Start by preheating the oven to 180°C/fan 160°C and having a small 25 x 20cm (2.6 litre) roasting/lasagne dish ready.

Put the cherries into the base of the dish with the sugar, cinnamon, cornflour and salt. Mix well.

Now mix the cake ingredients. Put the sugar, flour, cocoa, cinnamon, baking powder and salt in a bowl and combine.

Sprinkle the dry ingredients all over the fruit mix. Now drizzle over the melted butter and bake for 40–45 minutes.

I like to serve this piping hot, with dollops of chocolate ice cream.

serves 4–6 | prep 20 mins | cook 40–45 mins

citrus clove cake

This is much like a lemon drizzle in that it is a simple loaf cake with a crunchy, zesty top. But this version is laced with a combination of citrus fruits and paired with the subtle hint of clove. It's a real go-to cake for me, the kind that you put on a stand and the next time you look, it's all gone.

200g unsalted butter

200g soft brown sugar

1 teaspoon ground cloves

4 medium eggs

200g self-raising flour, sifted

1 lemon, zest and juice

1 orange, zest and juice

1 lime, zest and juice

120g caster sugar, for the crunchy top

Preheat the oven to 170°C/fan 150°C and line a 900g loaf tin.

Cream the butter and brown sugar together till light and fluffy. Mix in the ground cloves.

Add the eggs one by one till combined. Drop in the flour and lemon, orange and lime zest and mix till you have a smooth cake batter.

Pour the mixture into the tin, level off and bake for 35–40 minutes.

As soon as the cake comes out of the oven, use a cocktail stick or skewer to poke holes all over it. Mix the citrus juices with the caster sugar, pour the mixture all over the cake and leave to cool completely in the tin.

makes
8
slices

prep
10
mins

cook
40
mins

sumac plums

Simple desserts are often overlooked, but they need not be, and can be jazzed up using warming spices. I love these plums, which are roasted with the stones still in to give them maximum flavour. With vanilla fragrance and the sharpness of sumac, they are delicious served with yoghurt and some crushed amaretti biscuits.

400g plums

100g caster sugar

½ vanilla pod

2 teaspoons sumac

To serve

Greek yoghurt

sumac

amaretti biscuits

Preheat the oven to 180°C/fan 160°C.

Halve the plums with the stones still inside – they impart flavour so we will remove them later.

Put the plums in a roasting dish with the sugar. Scrape out the insides of the vanilla pod and add the seeds to the plums along with the pod. Sprinkle over the sumac and mix everything together.

Bake for 15–20 minutes till the plums are just soft. Take the dish out and remove the stones from the plums.

Serve three to four plum halves each with some yoghurt, a sprinkling of sumac and some crumbled amaretti biscuits. Drizzle over that plum juice.

serves
4–6

prep
10 mins

cook
15–20 mins

squash slabs

All cake should be eaten in slab form! Squash is sweet and bright and can be used for sweet as well as savoury recipes. This recipe is moist and has all the deliciousness you want in a slab of cake, topped with a thick layer of cream cheese icing.

For the cake

200ml oil, plus extra for greasing

225g soft brown sugar

4 medium eggs

1 orange, zest only

200g squash, grated

125g mixed nuts, roughly chopped

2 teaspoons mixed spice

225g self-raising flour

For the icing

150g full-fat cream cheese

50g unsalted butter

200g icing sugar

1 teaspoon vanilla bean paste

Preheat the oven to 150°C/fan 130°C and line and grease a 20 x 30cm rectangular tin.

Start by mixing the oil, sugar and eggs together. Now add the zest, squash and nuts and mix through.

Add the mixed spice and flour and mix till you have a glossy cake batter. Pour into the tin and bake in the oven for 40–45 minutes.

Once the cake is baked, leave to cool completely in the tin.

Make the icing by mixing the cream cheese and butter together till combined. Add the icing sugar and mix in well. Add the vanilla and mix through. Spread all over the cake and cut into slabs.

makes 16 slices

prep 15 mins

cook 40-45 mins

CHEESY

———

one-pan cheese and egg sandwich

As meals go, this is a whopper; perfect for a lazy Sunday morning or a late brunch. It has everything – bread, eggs and cheese – all cooked and folded in one pan, with tangy pickle and a warm, oozy centre. It's not just fun to eat, but fun to make too.

oil, for frying

4 medium eggs

a pinch of salt

1 teaspoon chilli flakes

a small handful of finely chopped fresh chives

2 slices of white bread

1 tablespoon chunky pickle

50g Red Leicester, finely grated

Start by pouring some oil into a large non-stick frying pan and heating over a medium heat.

Break the eggs into a bowl with the salt, chilli and chives and mix well.

Lower the heat of the oil and pour in the egg mixture, making sure you have an even layer.

Take your two slices of bread and lay them open so they are symmetrical. Place both slices of bread into the runny egg and leave till the egg is cooked. Flip onto a large plate or board, so the bread slices are no longer visible. Slide back onto the pan.

Spread the visibly shaped tops of the bread with pickle.

Flip the edges of the egg inwards over the pickle on all sides.

Add the cheese to one slice of bread, flip the other piece over it and leave to cook till the cheese has melted (about 2 minutes), making sure to press down with a fish slice to encourage the cheese to melt and stick the bread together, along with the egg.

Once the cheese has melted and beautifully welded the eggy bread, take the pan off the heat and give it a few minutes or you will burn your mouth, then cut and enjoy.

recipe photographs over page ▶

makes
1

prep
10 mins

cook
10 mins

ricotta blackberry breakfast cups

As a mother of two hungry teenagers and a little girly who grazes all day, I can tell you these are amazing for breakfast, filled with blackberries, while also convenient for a quick snack. They are zesty, fruity, wholesome and keep teenagers quiet for longer than a few minutes.

120g unsalted butter, softened, plus extra for greasing the tin

150g ricotta

180g soft brown sugar

1 medium egg

150g plain flour

150g porridge oats

1 teaspoon baking powder

1 lemon, zest only

150g blackberries

50g granola

For the yoghurt icing

200g yoghurt

100g icing sugar, sifted

a handful of blackberries (approx. 25g)

Preheat the oven to 180°C/fan 160°C and grease the inside of a 12-hole muffin tin.

Put the butter in a bowl with the ricotta and brown sugar and mix well. Add the egg and mix, then add the flour, oats, baking powder and lemon zest and mix well.

Divide the mixture into the 12 holes. Top with one or two black-berries per cup. Sprinkle over the granola and bake for 20–25 minutes. Leave to cool in the tin for 10 minutes, then take out.

Mix the yoghurt with the icing sugar, crush in just a few black-berries and ripple through. Drizzle over the cupcakes and they are ready to eat. Keep in the fridge in an airtight container for up to 3 days.

makes 12 · prep 20 mins · cook 25 mins

mac and cheesy

I have a dozen different ways to make mac and cheese and I happily share each version every chance I get. This is my kids' slightly psychedelic version, made using their favourite puffed cheesy crisps, which they used to devour as youngsters. The extra cheesiness and bright orange colour from the cheese puffs blitzed to a powder is mixed with the mac and topped with breadcrumbs. It's fun, it's delicious and it's bright!

400g macaroni pasta

30g unsalted butter

3 tablespoons plain flour (30g)

600ml whole milk

170ml evaporated milk

1 teaspoon yeast extract

450g Cheddar cheese, grated

2 tablespoons Worcestershire sauce

8 x 16.5g packs of cheese puffs, blended to a powder

For the top

50g breadcrumbs

cheese puff crumbs

50g Cheddar cheese, grated

Start by cooking the macaroni as per the instructions. When the macaroni is cooked, drain, rinse under cold water and set aside.

Preheat the oven to 200°C/fan 180°C.

Make the sauce by putting the butter in a saucepan and popping onto a medium heat. When the butter has melted, add the flour and whisk in. Add the milk a little at a time, whisking all the time until incorporated.

When the mixture begins to thicken, add the evaporated milk and yeast extract and cook until the mixture is thick. Take off the heat and allow to sit for 5 minutes.

Add the cheese to the sauce and mix in until melted. Stir in the Worcestershire sauce and half the cheese puffs, then add the macaroni and mix through. Tip it into an ovenproof dish and level off the top.

Sprinkle over the breadcrumbs, remaining cheese puffs and the grated cheese.

Bake for 30–35 minutes. Take out and leave for 10 minutes before eating.

serves 6–8   prep 25 mins   cook 45 mins

watercress soup with crispy goat's cheese

Growing up, we only ate watercress when Dad bought it from the yellow sticker aisle at closing time in the upmarket super-market near the restaurant he ran. It was green, it was edible, he was having it! We always stirred it into curries, usually with fish. This recipe is a world away from that but delicious all the same. Blitzed with fresh mint and cream, this smooth water-cress soup is then topped with crisp, fiery black-pepper-crusted goat's cheese.

For the soup

2 tablespoons olive oil

1 clove of garlic, minced

1 onion, diced

½ teaspoon salt

1 medium potato, peeled and cubed

500ml veg stock

2 lemons, 1 juiced, 1 cut into wedges to squeeze over

150g watercress

a small handful of fresh mint

100ml double cream

For the crispy goat's cheese

200g goat's cheese, cut into chunks (the rindless goat's cheese logs you can buy are easy to cut into chunks)

2 tablespoons ground black pepper

2–3 large eggs, beaten

75g breadcrumbs

vegetable, sunflower or rapeseed oil, for frying

Make the soup first by putting the oil in a medium saucepan. As soon as the oil is warm, add the garlic and warm through till golden. Add the onion and salt and cook for 10–15 minutes till the onion is soft and lightly caramelized.

Add the potato and cook for a few minutes till lightly brown. Pour in the stock and lemon juice, bring to the boil and leave to simmer for 10–15 minutes till the potato is cooked. Remove from the heat.

Meanwhile, make the crispy goat's cheese by tossing the cheese pieces in the black pepper. Roll around in the egg and then the breadcrumbs, and then do the same again.

Add 1cm oil to a sauté pan and heat over a medium heat. Have a plate ready with a few pieces of kitchen paper to drain the cheese of excess oil.

Fry the cheese in batches till golden all over, then drain (they puff up as they cook).

Add the lemon juice, watercress, mint and cream to the soup and blend with a stick blender. If the soup is very thick, add 150–250ml water and blend again. Reheat the soup for 1–2 minutes if needed.

To serve, pour the soup into bowls, squeeze over a little extra lemon, and top with a few pieces of goat's cheese and some black pepper.

serves 4 | prep 30 mins | cook 30 mins

cheesy chicken Kievs

Considered retro by some, personally I love a chicken Kiev, probably because we never ate them growing up, so I don't see them that way. I prefer to make them myself, and my Kievs are filled not only with garlic butter but also with gooey cheese, then coated and fried in Parmesan breadcrumbs. They can be made ahead – assembled 24 hours in advance, kept covered in the fridge, then cooked from chilled as per the recipe. I like to serve them with smooth mash and roasted tomatoes. I've also been known to slice any leftovers and stick in a wrap. I'm just saying . . .

For the filling

4 cloves of garlic, minced

2 tablespoons finely chopped fresh parsley

100g Parmesan, finely grated (or use a bag of pre-grated fresh Parmesan)

100g butter, softened

juice of ½ lemon

For the chicken

8 large chicken breast fillets

225g breadcrumbs

75g Parmesan, grated

5–6 large eggs, beaten

100g plain flour

1 tablespoon paprika

1 teaspoon salt

oil, for frying

Begin by making the filling. Put the garlic, parsley, Parmesan, butter and lemon juice in a food processor and blitz till well combined. Pop the blade out carefully and set the butter aside. (Alternatively, you could very easily buy some good garlic butter from the shops and bring to room temperature.)

Take the chicken fillets and use a sharp knife to create a hole in the thicker part of the breast, going down towards the narrower part to create a cavity. Do this to all eight.

Spoon the filling into each cavity, using a toothpick to secure the hole. Put into the fridge, covered, while you prepare the coating.

Mix the breadcrumbs and cheese on a large plate. Beat the eggs in a shallow bowl. Mix the flour, paprika and salt on another plate.

Take each chicken fillet and remove the toothpick. Dip into the flour, then the egg, then the breadcrumbs. Then the egg again and then the breadcrumbs again. Pop onto a plate and then do the same to the other seven. Leave them covered in the fridge for an hour (or up to 24 hours, or freeze at this stage).

Put some oil in a pan and preheat the oven to 180°C/fan 160°C.

When the oil is hot, gently fry the Kievs over a low heat till the breadcrumbs are golden and, as soon as they are, transfer onto a baking tray. Bake for 20–25 minutes. Serve with roasted tomatoes and creamy mashed potato.

serves 4

prep 30 mins + chilling

cook 30 mins

saag paneer pilau

Saag is greens, for which I like to use spinach but you can use whatever you fancy, and paneer is a delicious hard curd cheese, which is amazing at taking on flavour and doesn't change shape when cooked. Traditionally cooked as a curry, here I have added rice to the mix to make a one-pot easy pilau, giving you the most vibrant and flavourful pot of rice.

6 tablespoons ghee

4 teaspoons cumin seeds

4 cloves of garlic, minced

1 onion, grated

225g paneer, cut into cubes

150g spinach

juice of 1 lemon

2 teaspoons salt

400g basmati rice

800ml hot water

To serve 6 large eggs, at room temperature

pickled red cabbage

Start by putting the ghee in a large non-stick pan that must have a lid. As soon as the ghee is hot, add the cumin seeds and let them bubble away for 1 minute. Add the garlic and onion and cook over a medium to high heat for around 5 minutes until golden. Add the paneer and cook for 2–3 minutes till it is no longer pale and takes on a golden colour.

Blend the spinach to a paste using a splash of water. Add the spinach and lemon juice to the pan, season well with the salt and cook till the mixture is dry.

Add the rice and cook for 1–2 minutes. You will see it start to get a brighter white in the centre of the grains (if you look hard you will see the change, just ever so slightly).

Pour in the hot water and bring to the boil. As it boils, the liquid will reduce. When the water is thick and the rice visible (after about 5 minutes), reduce the heat to the lowest you can get it, cover and leave to steam for 30 minutes.

Meanwhile, soft-boil the eggs by dropping them into a pan of simmering water and cooking for 6 minutes.

After 30 minutes, take the lid off the pilau, leave for 10 minutes and it's ready to serve. I like to serve this with a sprinkling of pickled red cabbage and the soft-boiled eggs cut in half.

serves 6

prep 15 mins + resting

cook 50 mins

nachos bake

Nachos are our favourite movie snack, be it in front of the telly, at the cinema or just as a fun dinner. This is our literally beefed-up version. The beef mince is delicious flavoured with harissa, topped with tortilla chips straight out of a bag, sprinkled with cheese and grilled. Best served with all the toppings: jalapeños, guac, soured cream and coriander.

6 tablespoons oil

4 cloves of garlic, minced

2 onions, diced

1 teaspoon salt

2 teaspoons chilli powder

1 teaspoon ground cumin

1 teaspoon ground coriander

500g passata

3 tablespoons brown sauce (about 60g)

3 tablespoons Worcestershire sauce (45ml)

450g beef mince

200g tortilla chips

100g Cheddar cheese, grated

To serve jalapeños

guacamole

soured cream

a small bunch of fresh coriander, chopped

Start by adding the oil to a shallow casserole dish. As soon as the oil is hot, add the garlic and onion and cook through for about 10 minutes till soft and golden.

Add the salt, chilli, cumin and coriander and cook the spices for 1–2 minutes.

Pour in the passata, brown sauce and Worcestershire sauce, add the mince and cook for 10 minutes on a simmer.

As soon as it has thickened and the meat has cooked, preheat the oven to 220°C/fan 200°C.

Take the beef off the heat and scatter the tortilla chips on top. Sprinkle over the Cheddar and bake for about 5 minutes till the cheese has melted.

Take out and scatter over the jalapeños, dollop on the guacamole and soured cream and sprinkle over the coriander.

serves 6 | prep 20 mins | cook 30 mins

roast trio of cheeses

Let's just forget the traditional roast dinner for a moment please and celebrate the fact that here we are roasting three cheeses! These three different types, marinated and baked with vegetables, make for a delicious all-in-one-tray roast that is perfect for a simple yet delicious meat-free dinner. As if the baking of three cheeses isn't enough, they are drizzled and doused with bags of flavour.

500g new potatoes, halved

4 tablespoons oil

150g padron peppers

3 red onions, quartered

For the cheeses

250g halloumi

200g feta cheese

6 tablespoons oil

1 tablespoon chilli flakes

1 tablespoon dried thyme

3 tablespoons balsamic vinegar

a good pinch of salt

1 lemon, zest and juice

1 tablespoon pomegranate molasses

200g burrata

To serve

a handful of fresh parsley leaves

pomegranate molasses

50g pomegranate seeds

Preheat the oven to 220°C/fan 200°C.

Put the halved potatoes and a drizzle of oil into a roasting tin and roast for 10 minutes while you prep the other ingredients.

To marinate the cheeses, take the halloumi and feta and score/hedgehog both the tops without cutting all the way through.

Into a bowl add the oil, chilli, thyme, balsamic, salt, lemon zest and juice and the molasses and mix through. Add the three cheeses, cover in all that flavour and set aside.

Take your tin with the potatoes out of the oven, add the padron peppers and red onion and toss in the oil. Season and bake for 15 minutes.

Take out and make room in the centre, add the three cheeses, drizzle over the marinade, then bake for another 15 minutes.

Take out, sprinkle over the parsley, molasses and pomegranate seeds, and it's ready to serve.

serves 4 · prep 15 mins · cook 40 mins

rice
ice cream

My husband laughs at me for trying unusual foods because more often than not they are a disappointment, or at least way below expectations. He is a strawberry ice cream kind of guy, whether at home, the cinema or sat by the Trevi Fountain, eating scoops of the world's best gelato. Of all the flavours I could have chosen on a sunny day in Rome after a long walk, I decided to try the rice ice cream. But rather than complain about how much I didn't like it, I came home and made a better version: cooked rice flavoured with cardamom, mixed with a simple vanilla ice cream made from condensed milk and some cottage cheese for extra frozen bursts.

100g basmati rice

200ml water

6 cardamom pods, seeds removed

1 cinnamon stick

1 bay leaf

100ml milk

300ml double cream

397g tin of condensed milk

1 teaspoon vanilla bean paste

300g cottage cheese

Start by soaking the rice in cold water 2 days in advance. By soaking it, you really enhance the flavour of the rice. (At the very least, soak for a minimum of 1 hour.)

After soaking, drain the rice, add it to a processor with the water and the seeds of the cardamom pods and blitz till the rice is just broken.

Pour into a small pan, add the cinnamon stick and bay leaf and bring to the boil. As soon as it does, stir until thickened. Cover and leave to steam for 10 minutes (the rice needs to be well cooked and soft at this stage as it hardens in the freezer).

Remove from the heat, transfer to a bowl to cool and take out the bay and cinnamon. Pour in the milk, stir to separate out any rice clumps, and set aside to cool totally.

Add the cream to another bowl with the condensed milk and vanilla and whisk for 5–10 minutes till thickened. Add the cottage cheese and mix till combined.

Add the rice to the cream and mix through. Transfer to a plastic container, press baking parchment on the surface, cover with a lid and pop into the freezer for a minimum of 4 hours. If the ice cream has been frozen overnight, put in the fridge for at least 1 hour before serving so it is soft enough to scoop.

makes
1.5 litres

prep
25 mins + freezing

cook
50 mins

apple and Wensleydale pie

Cheese and fruit work really well together on a cheese board, so why not in a pie? That's where all good recipes are born: with the question, 'Why not?' The apples are spiced simply with cinnamon and the pie is dotted with Wensleydale, which has cranberries already in it. It's sweet, it's salty and it's fruity all at once!

For the pastry

400g plain flour, plus extra for dusting

2 tablespoons icing sugar

200g unsalted butter, cubed

4–5 tablespoons water

1 egg, lightly beaten

sugar, for sprinkling

For the filling

3 Bramley apples (about 500g in weight)

50g light soft brown sugar

2 tablespoons cornflour

20g pecans, roughly chopped

100g Wensleydale cheese with cranberries, broken into chunks

Start by making the pastry. Put the flour and icing sugar into a food processor. Add the butter and whizz until there are no big lumps of butter. Add 4 tablespoons of the water and pulse till the pastry starts to come together. If the mix is dry, add more water, 1 teaspoon at a time. As soon as the pastry does come together, tip it out and bring together into a round flat, wrap in cling film and leave to chill for 30 minutes.

Now make the filling. No pre-cooking needed – just mix together. Peel, core and chop the apples into bite-size pieces, pop into the centre of a tea towel and bring the edges together. Give the apples a squeeze and remove the moisture, or as much as you can. Tip into a bowl and add the sugar, cornflour, pecans and cheese, mix really well, then set aside.

Take an 8-inch (20cm) x 4cm deep round pie dish or pie plate. Preheat the oven to 200°C/fan 180°C.

Take the dough out of the fridge and cut off two-thirds. Roll out this piece of pastry so it is large enough to cover the base and sides and has a little overhang.

Pour the apple mixture into the pastry and level off.

Take the remaining third of the pastry and roll out a lid to fit the top. Brush the edges of the pastry with the beaten egg and add the top. Trim off the edges and cut a hole in the centre to release any steam. Use any extra pastry to create decorations. Glaze the top with the egg, sprinkle over the sugar and bake for 40–45 minutes until golden brown.

recipe photographs over page ▶

serves
6

prep
30 mins
+ chilling

cook
45 mins

carrot bundt cake

This bundt has all the deliciousness of a carrot cake, with spices, sweet carrot and cream cheese, but instead of frosting, all of that goodness is layered inside, rippled gently through the batter and baked in one bundt tin.

For the cake

170ml sunflower oil, plus extra for greasing

440g light soft brown sugar

4 large eggs

270g carrots, finely grated

280g plain flour, sifted

2 teaspoon baking powder

½ teaspoon salt

1 teaspoon ground cinnamon

1 teaspoon mixed spice

1 teaspoon ground nutmeg

For the cream cheese ripple

100g full-fat cream cheese

20g unsalted butter, softened

180g icing sugar

3 tablespoons milk

1 teaspoon vanilla bean extract

icing sugar, for dusting

Preheat the oven to 190°C/fan 170°C and grease the inside of a bundt tin well.

Put the oil, sugar, eggs and carrot in a bowl and mix well.

Add the flour and baking powder, salt, cinnamon, mixed spice and nutmeg to a separate bowl and mix till incorporated. Add to the wet ingredients and mix till you have an even batter.

Make the cream cheese ripple by whisking the cream cheese, butter, icing sugar, milk and vanilla bean extract together till combined.

Pour half the carrot cake batter into the tin and level off. Add the cream cheese on top, then add the rest of the carrot cake batter in a final layer. Use a skewer to ripple the batter.

Bake for 50 minutes–1 hour until the cake is risen and firm and a skewer inserted into the middle comes out clean.

Take out and leave to cool in the tin for at least 20 minutes so that the cake is firm enough to turn out.

Use a table knife or small palette knife to gently loosen the edges of the cake, then turn out. Once cooled, dust with icing sugar and serve. Will keep in the fridge for up to 5 days.

makes
10–12 slices

prep
30 mins

cook
1 hour

burnt Basque cheesecake

There are so many ways to make cheesecake and I think it's always a great thing to add another recipe to the repertoire. In some ways this is a cheesecake like any other – creamy, dense and eaten in wedges – but is baked in a hotter oven to give its signature burnt exterior. For anyone with a reputation for burning food, this is for you, but this time it's deliberate!

butter, for greasing the tin

900g full-fat cream cheese

360g caster sugar

6 medium eggs, lightly beaten

500ml cream

50g plain flour

Start by preheating the oven to 220°C/fan 200°C. Line and grease a 23 x 10cm deep round loose-bottomed cake tin. Make sure the paper is about 4cm above the top of the tin – this cheesecake rises a lot during cooking but then drops as it cools.

Whisk the cream cheese and sugar in a freestanding mixer or using an electric whisk for 2 minutes till well combined.

Pour the eggs in gradually while whisking and make sure they too are combined well. Add the cream and plain flour and mix in.

Pour the mixture into the tin, tapping the tin to remove any air bubbles (if there are any on the surface, pop with a toothpick).

Bake for 55–60 minutes. The cheesecake rises high in the tin and will look wobbly. It will sink and firm up as it sets.

Once baked, open the oven door and leave in there till the oven is completely cold. Take out and leave to chill in its tin in the fridge overnight – only then will it be ready to eat.

The simplicity of a cheesecake like this is that it needs nothing and is delicious as it is, but feel free to use it as your canvas to top with stewed fruit, compote, salted caramel, the list is endless . . .

serves 10 | prep 20 mins + chilling | cook 1 hour

NUTTY

mixed nut flapjack clusters

These are much like flapjacks, but with all the oaty, nutty elements of breakfast, and who said we can't have flapjacks for breakfast! Sweet and twice-cooked to create the crunchy clusters, they are perfect eaten with hot milk poured on top or crumbled into yoghurt.

250g chopped mixed nuts

250g rolled oats

250g unsalted butter, plus extra for greasing the tray

180g golden syrup

180g light brown sugar

1 teaspoon vanilla extract

1 teaspoon almond extract

100g mixed cereals

a good pinch of salt

a handful of dried sour cherries (optional)

Preheat the oven to 180°C/fan 160°C. Grease a large baking tray with sides, the biggest you have.

To the baking tray add the chopped nuts in a thin layer with the oats on top in another layer. Bake in the oven for 10 minutes.

Meanwhile, put the butter, syrup and brown sugar in a pan and turn on to a medium heat. Warm till the butter has melted and the sugar dissolved. You should have a dark brown even mixture. Take off the heat, add the vanilla and almond extract and mix.

Take the toasted nuts and oats out of the oven and pop into a large bowl. Add the butter mixture into it and mix till everything is evenly coated.

Add the mixed-up cereal, mix again, and lay into the prepared tin in an uneven manner. There's no need to level it off too much as this will allow it to bake unevenly, creating crunchy and chewy texture. Bake for 15 minutes. Leave to cool in the tin until it is cool enough to handle.

Take out, break apart into uneven chunks and separate the mixture out between two lined baking trays. Bake for another 10–15 minutes until a deeper golden colour.

Leave to cool completely in the trays and then it is ready to eat with hot or cold milk poured over for breakfast. I like a few dried sour cherries to go with it.

makes
30

prep
20 mins
+ cooling

cook
40 mins

brioche custard French toast

This is my emergency French toast for when I am out of eggs, which isn't often, but as a family we do get through them fast, and once we're down to two or three, that isn't even enough to feed the cat. But every problem has a solution. I don't let a lack of eggs stop us from having French toast, so this is made with – yes! – custard powder. And I love to use brioche, because why not? It's served with a pistachio maple drizzle.

For the pistachio maple drizzle

100g pistachios, plus extra for serving

150ml maple syrup

a pinch of salt

For the French toast

50g custard powder

30g icing sugar

225ml whole milk

1 teaspoon vanilla bean paste

8 thickly cut slices of brioche (about 40g a slice)

75g butter, softened

To serve

200g strawberries, halved

icing sugar, for dusting

Start by making the pistachio maple drizzle. Place the pistachios in a food processor and blitz to a fine dust. Add the maple syrup and blitz till fully combined. Add the pinch of salt. Transfer to a serving dish and set aside.

Now on to the French toast. Put the custard powder in a bowl along with the sugar and whisk to combine. Add the milk and vanilla and whisk till you have no more lumps left.

Take the slices of thick brioche and dip them in one by one, briefly on both sides, and pop onto a plate. Do this till you have used up all the custard mixture.

Get a large non-stick pan and put over a medium heat. Add a large knob of the butter to the pan and wait for it to melt. As soon as it's melted and there is enough butter covering the base in a decent layer, pop the first brioche slice in. The pan needs to be hot when the brioche goes in, so reduce the heat to low as soon as the brioche is in and fry in the butter on a medium heat for 2–3 minutes, keeping a close eye to make sure it doesn't burn. Turn over and cook for 1–2 minutes on the other side. It should be evenly coloured and golden where the sugar has melted.

Do this to each one, making sure to add enough butter each time to fry the slices. If you are using a large non-stick pan, you can cook them in batches of three to four. Wipe out the butter from the pan in between batches to avoid burnt butter.

Serve the hot French toast with fresh strawberries and a drizzle of that delicious pistachio maple drizzle, then add a few extra chopped pistachios to go on top. Dust with icing sugar to finish, if you like.

serves 4 makes 8 toasts

prep 15 mins

cook 10 mins per batch

Bombay patty burgers

Burgers are the thing in our house and with two teenage boys, any variation is always welcomed. I didn't get a resounding whoop the first time I said we were having veggie burgers, but these ones changed their minds. Why? Because they offer big mouthfuls of meaty burger without the meat. The secret ingredients are Bombay mix and nuts, and for me the best bit is watching others try to work out what they are made of!

For the patties

200g Bombay mix, plus extra for serving

100g spicy coated nuts

300ml boiling water

1½ tablespoons chaat masala

1 medium egg, beaten

oil, for greasing the tray

4 x 5mm slices of a large red onion

a pinch of salt

To serve

4 spicy cheese slices

4 brioche burger buns or mini naans

4 tablespoons mayonnaise

lime pickle

Start by putting the Bombay mix and nuts in a food processor and blitzing until they form an uneven, crumby mixture.

Add the boiling water to that, mix and leave for 15 minutes for the liquid to soak in.

Preheat the oven to 180°C/fan 160°C.

Add the chaat masala to the mix and stir in well, then add the egg and combine well.

Grease a baking tray that has sides, line with some baking paper and grease the paper on top too. Lay the four slices of onion in the tray and season lightly.

Divide the Bombay mix and nut mixture into four patties using wet hands and pop onto the tray. Make sure they are just flattened slightly. Bake for 25 minutes.

Take the patties out, add the cooked onion on top of each patty and a slice of cheese. Put the brioche buns on the same tray to warm up, then pop back into the oven for a few minutes till the cheese has melted.

To assemble, lay out the burger buns, smother the bases with mayonnaise, then pop the patties with the onion and cheese on each base.

Smother the top with lime pickle and then sprinkle over some more Bombay mix. Finish with the burger bun tops and they are ready to eat!

serves 4

prep 20 mins + soaking

cook 30 mins

savoury baklava

To any purists, I would apologize, but actually I can't because these are insanely out-of-this-world good. Filo, layered with butter, filled halfway with a nutty, cheesy chipotle mixture, covered in more buttered filo and then topped with cheese and baked till golden, these make for the ultimate lunch served with a simple salad, or eaten cold out of the fridge (which I do, often!).

65g unsalted butter, melted

270g pack of filo pastry

250g mixed nuts

1–2 tablespoons chipotle chilli flakes

1 tablespoon onion granules

200ml hot water, mixed with 1 vegetable stock cube

1 large spring onion, thinly sliced

200g Gruyère cheese, grated

green salad and honey mustard dressing, to serve

Preheat the oven to 180°C/fan 160°C. Grease the inside, base and sides of a loose-bottomed, if you have one, 24cm square tin with a little of the melted butter.

Cut the filo in half so you have 14 sheets. Take one sheet of filo and pop inside the tin. Grease the sheet and add another, rotating the tin as you go so that you have covered the base and all four sides. Grease the sheet, add another and keep doing this till you have done 7 sheets.

Now on to the nutty centre. Put the nuts in a food processor and blitz until they form a fine crumb mixture. Add the blitzed nuts to a bowl with the chilli flakes, onion granules and hot water and mix together. Add the spring onion and 150g of the cheese and mix well.

Pour the nutty centre onto the top of the filo base and spread all over evenly. Now add a sheet of the filo, butter all over and add another sheet, scrunching them a little as you add them so they fit in the tin, till you have used all 7 sheets. Make sure you butter the top sheet as well.

Cut into four equal squares and add a mound of the remaining grated cheese on top of each square. Bake for 30–35 minutes.

Leave to cool for 10 minutes before serving with a simple garden salad tossed with a honey mustard dressing to complement the baklava.

serves 4

prep 25 mins

cook 35 mins

peanut butter egg curry

An egg curry was something we normally ate at home when Mum's dozen other curries were depleted. But an egg curry can shine all on its own – it needn't be the understudy or Plan B to something better. Oh no! This curry is packed with flavour and finished with peanut butter for the smoothest sauce ever.

6 – 8 duck eggs

6 tablespoons oil

50g unsalted peanuts

1 bay leaf

1 large dried chilli

1 tablespoon coriander seeds, crushed

6 cloves of garlic, minced

2 onions, grated

1 teaspoon salt

2 teaspoons tomato paste

2 teaspoons tamarind

3 tomatoes, grated

1 tablespoon curry powder

85g peanut butter

300ml hot water

60g watercress, finely chopped

Hard-boil the duck eggs for 10 minutes in a pan of boiling water, then remove from the heat and peel when cool.

Start by pouring the oil into a shallow non-stick pan. Heat the oil on a medium to high heat. Now make sure each egg is dried of any liquid using kitchen paper. Drop the eggs into the hot oil and encourage them to move around to be scorched and bubble the texture. This should take about 5 minutes and will help the sauce stick to the egg rather than just slide off. Once they are browned and textured all over, remove from the pan.

Now add your peanuts to the pan and toast for a minute till golden, along with the bay leaf and chilli.

Add the crushed coriander seeds and allow to sizzle. Add the garlic and as soon as the garlic is golden, add the grated onion. Cook on a medium heat for about 10 minutes until the onion is golden brown and caramelized.

Now add the salt, tomato paste, tamarind and grated tomatoes and cook till the mixture is dry. Add the curry powder, peanut butter and hot water and leave to simmer till the oil bubbles rise to the top. This should take about 10 minutes.

Add the watercress and stir in till wilted. Add the eggs back in and mix through. It is ready to eat. I like to eat this with rice or naan bread.

serves 4–6 prep 30 mins cook 50 mins

walnut and lamb nogadas

I discovered these in a market whilst away travelling. Stuffed peppers do often have a bad rep, but these ones are a bit different, in fact a lot different, with the peppers roasted till sweet and unctuous, then laid flat and covered with a layer of za'atar spiced mince and a drizzling of garlicky, charred walnut sauce. So forget stuffed peppers, here the only things that will be stuffed are me and you!

2 peppers, a mixture of yellow and red

1 large bulb of garlic

1 pack of spring onions, rooty ends removed

oil, for drizzling

For the lamb

3 tablespoons oil

100g walnuts, roughly chopped

3 cloves of garlic, minced

1 tablespoon chilli flakes

400g tin of chopped tomatoes

1 teaspoon salt

2 tablespoons vinegar

2 tablespoons za'atar

450g lamb mince

For the sauce

100g walnuts

300ml single cream

a pinch of salt

To serve

za'atar

pomegranate seeds

a squeeze of lime juice

Preheat the oven to 220°C/fan 200°C.

Put the peppers, garlic and spring onions on a large baking tray, drizzle generously with oil and massage in. As soon as the oven is hot, add the peppers and leave till the peppers are black and scorched. This will take about 20 –25 minutes.

Meanwhile, start on the lamb. Pour the oil into a saucepan and heat on a low heat. Add the walnuts and toast gently for 1–2 minutes. Add the garlic and chilli and cook till the garlic is brown.

Pour in the chopped tomatoes, salt and vinegar, then cook for a few minutes. Add the za'atar and minced lamb and cook for 10 minutes, then leave on the lowest heat to simmer for 45–50 minutes until the mixture is quite dry.

Take the roasted charred veg out of the oven and pop the peppers into a zip-sealed bag to steam. Seal and leave for 20 minutes to steam off the outer skin. Have a large platter or plate at the ready.

Make the sauce by putting the walnuts in a food processor with the roughly chopped charred spring onions. Extract the garlic cloves from the charred flesh and pop straight into the processor too. Blitz to a smooth paste. Add the cream, season and give it one final whizz to combine. If the sauce is thick, add a splash of water to loosen.

Take the peppers out of the bag and leave for a few minutes until cool enough to handle. Remove the thin outer skin, cut in half down one side, remove the seeds and stem and open. Lay the peppers out flat on the platter or plate. Take spoonfuls of the mince mixture and place on the insides of the peppers.

serves 6 · prep 40 mins · cook 1 hr 10 mins

Drizzle over the sauce generously and serve any extra alongside. Sprinkle over the za'atar and pomegranate seeds and squeeze that lime over.

no-waste creamy carbonara

When I make carbonara, I always get into a tizz about what to do with the leftover egg whites, and often I have too many in the freezer, always some sat in the fridge and meringues I just don't know what to do with. So this recipe is perfect for when you want to make carbonara but definitely don't need the waste. The egg whites are turned into a mock 'bacon' using smoked paprika, while the yolks are mixed with tahini to create that smooth, creamy, luxurious coating. Not only is it yum, it's also vegetarian!

300g spaghetti

3 tablespoons olive oil

4 medium eggs, separated

2 teaspoons smoked paprika

½ teaspoon salt

150g frozen peas

For the sauce

3 tablespoons tahini

1 teaspoon ground black pepper

Start by cooking the pasta as per the instructions on the packet.

Pour the oil into a pan and heat to a high heat. In a bowl, mix the egg whites with the paprika and salt and whisk really well.

Keep the heat up on the pan and add the egg white mix in. Whisk and cook till the mixture is scrambled. Let it then sit on the base on a high heat for 3 seconds – we want it to catch just a little to enhance the smoky flavour. Stir and break up.

Before draining the pasta, add the frozen peas and cook for just a minute. Drain the pasta, reserving a few ladles of that starchy water.

Add the drained pasta to the egg pieces and stir through on a medium heat. Lower the heat.

Mix the egg yolk and tahini. Don't worry if it seizes, the pasta water will help to loosen it again. Add to the spaghetti and mix through. Add a ladle of that starchy pasta water and mix till you have a creamy sauce that has coated the spaghetti. Enjoy hot, and if you fancy some cheese, sprinkle with a little of that cheesy goodness, along with the ground black pepper.

serves 4 / prep 15 mins / cook 15 mins

chia chicken

For me, there is nothing worse than a mediocre, limp, lifeless salad, so if I make a salad, it has to have everything, it has to *be* everything! This is that salad. It has a nutty chia pesto that enrobes crisped-up shreds of chicken and fried tortellini. It has bags of flavour: nutty, slightly cheesy, crunchy and crisp!

200g precooked chicken breast

100g cherry tomatoes, halved

600g tortellini

oil, for frying

a pinch of salt

a small handful of salad leaves

For the chia pesto (makes 335g)

50g chia seeds

30g fresh parsley

30g fresh basil

50g Parmesan cheese, finely grated (or use pre-grated to make it quicker)

150ml olive oil

2 cloves of garlic

2 tablespoons balsamic vinegar

salt and ground black pepper

Start by making the chia pesto. Put the chia seeds, parsley, basil, Parmesan, olive oil, garlic and balsamic vinegar in a food processor and blitz to a smooth pesto. Check the seasoning and adjust if you need to. Once made, set aside.

Shred the precooked chicken into a large bowl. Add the halved tomatoes and mix together.

Now to the tortellini. Add about 2–3cm of oil to a medium saucepan and heat on a medium heat.

Have a plate lined with kitchen paper. In batches, fry the tortellini, turning them in the oil till they are lightly golden and crisp on both sides. Drain by lifting onto the paper with a slotted spoon. You can do this in about six batches, at 2–3 minutes per batch. Once they are all cooked and crisp, sprinkle with salt to keep crisp.

Add the tortellini to the chicken mix and stir through. Add the salad leaves and pesto and toss through. It is now ready to eat.

serves 4–6   prep 20 mins   cook 15 mins

chocolate salami

This is much like tiffin, in fact it is tiffin, but dressed differently, and why not. Chunks of shortbread, rich macadamia nuts, ginger, orange and dark chocolate are all rolled up into a salami shape, dusted and served in slices. Now you can make something beautiful, tasty and a little bit fancy-looking without even turning on the oven.

180g shortbread biscuits

80g macadamia nuts

20g stem ginger

1 orange, zest only

½ teaspoon sea salt flakes

200g dark chocolate, chopped

90g unsalted butter

90ml whole milk

icing sugar, for dusting

Roughly chop the biscuits into uneven pieces. Do the same with the nuts, put in a bowl and mix together. Chop the stem ginger into fine, even pieces and add to the bowl along with the orange zest and salt. Mix well.

Put the chocolate, butter and milk into a small pan and melt till you have an even, glossy mixture. Leave to cool to room temperature or it will make the biscuits soggy, then add the chocolate to the biscuit mix and stir until everything is combined.

Take a large sheet of cling film and double it up. Add the mixture lengthways to the centre, spreading it across about 20cm in a log shape. Use the cling film to help roll the mixture into a sausage shape, then twist the ends to make sure it is secure. Pop into the fridge for a few hours.

Roll the salami every time you go into the fridge so that as it cools it maintains that rounded shape. Leave overnight.

Before taking out of the cling film, roll the salami again to ensure a round log shape. Remove from the cling film and dust generously with icing sugar all over, brushing any excess off. Leave for a few minutes so it's not too brittle when cutting, then slice. It is ready to eat with a delicious hot drink. The salami will keep in the fridge for up to one week.

makes
10
slices

prep
20 mins
+ chilling

cook
5
mins

pretzel nut brûlée

When my brother tried this he declared, 'This is my new favourite,' but let's just say that changes, often! It's my version of a custard tart, with a smooth baked centre, but it's what's underneath and on top that really makes it special. The pastry is made with hazelnuts and salted pretzels that give it a crunchy nuttiness; and once baked the custard is covered with sugar and blow-torched to create a crisp, sugary brûlée topping.

For the tart shell

50g blanched hazelnuts

50g salted pretzels

200g plain flour

150g unsalted butter, cubed and cold

2 tablespoons cold water

For the filling

500ml double cream

75g caster sugar, plus an extra 40g for the top

9 egg yolks (save some egg white for glazing)

Start by making the pastry for the tart shell. Blitz the nuts and pretzels in a food processor to a fine crumb. Add the flour and quickly whizz to combine. Then add the butter and allow the mixture to clump. Add the water and blitz till the pastry comes together. If it is too dry, add an extra teaspoon of water at a time.

Take the pastry out of the processor, wrap in cling film and leave to chill in the fridge for half an hour.

Have a 25cm fluted loose-bottom tart tin at the ready. Take the pastry out of the fridge and roll it out between sheets of cling film so you can get it as thin as possible and large enough to cover the base and sides of your tin, with some overhang. Lift off the top piece of cling film and use the base cling film to gently flip the pastry on top of the tin. Peel away the cling film and push the pastry into the base and fluted edges of the tin. Trim off all the excess, then poke holes into the base using a fork and pop into the freezer for 30 minutes.

Preheat the oven to 180°C/fan 160°C and pop a baking tray onto the middle shelf.

Take the lined tin out of the freezer, add a scrunched-up piece of baking paper into the tart shell and fill with baking beans or dry lentils. Pop onto a hot baking tray and bake for 20 minutes.

After 20 minutes, take out the tart shell, including the tray, and remove the paper and beans. Return it to the oven to bake for 10 minutes without the paper, then brush it with the leftover egg white and cook for another 2 minutes.

Take the tart shell out and leave on a rack to cool. Reduce the oven temperature to 150°C/fan 130°C.

Now on to the filling. Pour the cream into a saucepan and bring just to the boil, then take off the heat. Add the sugar and egg yolks to a medium bowl and whisk well till combined. Gently pour the hot cream into the egg mixture in a steady stream, whisking all the time.

Pour the filling into the baked tart shell through a sieve to catch any eggy lumps that might have formed. This will result in a super-smooth baked custard. Pop any bubbles on the surface using a toothpick.

Pop back into the oven and bake for 35–40 minutes. When you take it out there will be a slight wobble in the centre.

Leave to cool in the tin completely and then refrigerate for at least 4 hours. Once you are ready to serve, sprinkle the remaining sugar evenly across the top, avoiding the pastry edges. Using a blowtorch, heat the sugar till golden all over and leave to set for a few minutes. It is now ready to remove from the tin and slice.

serves
4

prep
30 mins
+ chilling

cook
1 hr
15 mins

chestnut torta

Packed with toasted nuts, this dense torta is perfect for a chocolate fix – something we all need from time to time. Enhanced with a touch of coffee, it's wonderfully rich and indulgent. Pull on your woolly socks, cosy up and enjoy a slice served with cream and jam – like a fuss-free afternoon tea in a bowl.

50g plain flour

50g ground almonds

200g unsalted butter, plus extra for greasing the tin

200g dark chocolate, chopped

1 teaspoon instant coffee

4 medium eggs

200g caster sugar

100g chestnuts, roughly chopped

100g roasted hazelnuts. roughly chopped

To serve icing sugar

cocoa powder

cream

jam

Start by putting the flour and ground almonds in a non-stick frying pan and toasting on a low heat till golden. Take off the heat when golden and leave to cool completely in a bowl.

Put the butter, chocolate and coffee in a saucepan and melt on a low heat till it comes together into an even, glossy mixture. Leave to cool.

Preheat the oven to 180°C/fan 160°C. Grease and line the base and sides of a 23cm springform tin.

Add the eggs and sugar to the cooled chocolate mixture and whisk on high using an electric whisk or in a freestanding mixer until combined. Add a third of the chocolate mixture to the flour mix and stir till really well combined. Add this back into the chocolate mix and fold through evenly.

Sprinkle the chestnuts first and then the hazelnuts into the base, then pour in the cake mix and level off the top. Bake for 40 minutes.

Leave the torta to cool in the tin till it's just warm and then take out. Take a small sieve, add cocoa to one side and icing sugar to the other and then dust the top all over. Serve in wedges with cream and jam.

serves 8–10

prep 20 mins

cook 50 mins

cinnamon sweet pesto

This is pesto, just a little bit reinvented – or in fact a lot, since it's sweet and there is no pasta in sight. Made with nuts, chocolate, spices and coconut, this, like any pesto, is a bung-it-in-the-processor type situation. Perfect for a quick dessert, served alongside a rainbow of tropical fruit and biscuits, it's easy but impressive and a bit of a crowd-pleaser.

100g pine nuts

120g white chocolate, plus extra shavings

40ml coconut oil

½ teaspoon ground cinnamon

30g coconut chips, toasted

To serve

sliced mango

sliced kiwis

strawberries

raspberries

blackberries

madeleines

shortbread

cigarrillo wafer biscuits

Preheat the oven to 160°C/fan 140°C. Start by toasting the pine nuts in the oven for 10 minutes. Leave to cool and then add to a food processor and blitz to a fine crumb.

Now melt the chocolate, add the coconut oil and mix till melted. Add the pine nuts and cinnamon and mix well. Arrange in a serving dish.

Toast the coconut chips over a low heat in a non-stick frying pan for 2–3 minutes, stirring constantly. Sprinkle the toasted coconut chips and chocolate shavings over the dip.

Surround the bowl with an array of colourful fruit, cakes and biscuits and serve.

serves 6–8

prep 10 mins

cook 20 mins

ZESTY

avo lime butter on toast

This 'butter' is zesty and perfect if you love avocado and want to eat it in a different way. Zingy, smooth and sweet, it's simple to make, and great spread on a bit of toasted sourdough, topped with salty smoked salmon and sesame seeds. This butter wears many hats, as not only can it be spread, but it can also be tossed through hot cooked pasta or used as a dip.

2 avocados

1 lime, zest and juice

2 tablespoons coconut oil

2 tablespoons maple syrup, plus extra to finish

a large pinch of salt

4 slices of bread

100g smoked salmon

2 teaspoons sesame seeds

Make the butter by putting the avocados into a food processor. Add the zest of the lime and the juice. Add the coconut oil, maple syrup and seasoning and whizz till it is a smooth paste.

Toast the bread on both sides.

Spread the toast with the avocado butter, layer the smoked salmon on top, then sprinkle the sesame seeds over it. Drizzle over a little bit of the maple syrup to finish with an extra touch of sweetness.

serves
4

prep
15 mins

cook
5 mins

Russian egg salad

I lived on egg salads throughout my first pregnancy. Then I had to avoid them for a while because twice a day for four months was becoming a problem. This recipe reminds me of why I loved them, as it's packed with everything my pregnant mouth desired: garlic, creamy egg yolks, sharp pickles and delicious mayo. Not forgetting my all-time fave: potatoes. (The pregnancy craving ended with a beautiful boy, but weirdly that boy is not so keen on potato salad! All the more for me.) This makes a great side dish.

500g potatoes, peeled and diced into 3cm chunks

6 carrots, peeled, halved lengthways, then sliced into 1cm half moons

6 medium eggs

200g frozen peas

2 cloves of garlic, minced

1 pickled egg

1 pickled onion, finely chopped

1 gherkin, diced

20g capers, roughly chopped

a large handful of fresh dill

300g crème fraîche

100g mayonnaise

a pinch of salt

Put the potatoes in a large pan with the carrots and eggs, cover with water and bring to the boil. After 8 minutes of boiling, remove the eggs and dunk into a bowl of cold water. Continue to simmer the potatoes and carrots for another 2 minutes until the potatoes are just cooked.

Drop the peas in for 30 seconds. Drain and rinse.

Put the potatoes, carrots and peas in a bowl and leave to cool completely. If you want to speed this process up you can cool them on a large tray, but that does mean more washing up. Your call!

Peel the eggs, chop each into eight pieces and add them to the bowl. Gently give it all a good mix.

Put the garlic in a smaller bowl, grate in the pickled egg and add the pickled onion, diced gherkin and capers. Mix with the dill, crème fraîche, mayonnaise and salt.

Add to the cooled vegetables and gently mix, then it's ready to serve.

serves 6–8 prep 20 mins + chilling cook 15 mins

orange ceviche

Ceviche isn't as fancy as one might think, and if we can get our head around sushi and sashimi, then I'm sure we can cure some fish in flavourful acid and enjoy it without feeling weird or pretentious. The thin slices of haddock are 'cooked' in citrus – it's magic and spectacular. Perfectly balanced sharpness best eaten simply with pitta chips.

For the ceviche

500g fresh haddock fillets, thinly sliced

2 limes, zest and juice

2 oranges, zest and juice

1 red onion, thinly sliced

1 red chilli, diced

2 tomatoes, deseeded and thinly sliced

30g fresh coriander, chopped

50ml olive oil

For the pitta chips

4 pitta breads

50ml olive oil

a pinch of salt

Start by putting the fish on a flat tray or dish in an even layer. Pour over the zest and juice of the limes and oranges and mix in with the fish. Cover and leave in the fridge for 2 hours.

Make the pitta chips. Preheat the oven to 180°C/fan 160°C.

Cut the pitta breads through the middle to separate them into two thin ovals. Rip these into uneven pieces so you have bits that are extra-crisp in parts.

Toss with the olive oil and a little salt. Spread out on a lined baking tray and bake for 10–15 minutes until golden and crisp.

After 2 hours, drain the fish to remove the liquid.

Put the onion in a serving bowl with the chilli, tomato and coriander and mix together. Add the fish and gently toss through. Serve with the pitta chips.

serves 4

prep 30 mins + chilling

cook 20 mins

lemon lamb with jewelled couscous

We all need a whopper of a recipe in our repertoire, and when I do roasts, my kids prefer lamb. So I always go for a big piece of butterflied lamb. Here the meat is covered in a zingy mix of preserved lemon and ras-el-hanout, baked in the oven, and then popped onto a cosy bed of couscous and baked again, ready to slice up and serve.

For the lamb

350g jar of preserved lemons, drained

3 tablespoons runny honey

65g ras-el-hanout

200ml oil, plus extra to serve

a pinch of salt

750g butterflied leg of lamb

For the couscous

150g baby spinach leaves

250g couscous

100g pine nuts

a pinch of saffron strands

a large bunch of fresh coriander, roughly chopped

80g pomegranate seeds

Preheat the oven to 180°C/fan 160°C and have a tray large enough to lay the leg of lamb in comfortably. Place the spinach into the base of the tray.

Halve the preserved lemons and remove the seeds, but be sure to keep the flesh in. Put in a blender along with the honey, ras-el-hanout, oil and salt and blend until smooth.

Pour the mixture all over the leg of lamb on both sides and roast for 30 minutes.

Remove the tray from the oven and add the couscous, pine nuts and saffron, mixing them in with the spinach. Pour in just enough water to cover the couscous and put the leg of lamb back on top.

Cook for another 20 minutes.

Remove the tray from the oven, take out the leg of lamb and leave to rest.

Fluff the couscous up with a fork and transfer onto a platter.

Slice up the leg of lamb and place on top of the couscous. Sprinkle over the coriander and pomegranate seeds, drizzle with a little olive oil and it's ready to serve.

serves 4

prep 20 mins

cook 50 mins

beef citrus rendang

I ate rendang for the first time at a restaurant that cooked fusion Thai and Chinese food and it was so delicious we ate it in silence, even though we were in a loud, crowded restaurant, and that says a lot about my family, because we can certainly talk. So, I just had to make my own version, and here it is, with thin slices of beef tenderly cooked in a deep, rich, dark sauce with the citrus hit of limes and lime leaves. I like to serve it with my cheat's puff-pastry parathas.

2 tablespoons oil

50g desiccated coconut

4 dried chillies

2 onions, diced

1 teaspoon salt

4 cloves of garlic, crushed

5cm ginger, peeled and crushed

4 lime leaves, chopped

4 limes, zest and juice

450g beef sirloin, very thinly sliced

100ml stock

160ml coconut cream

For parathas 500g puff pastry block

To serve a small handful of fresh coriander

25g toasted coconut

Pour the oil into a saucepan. When hot, add the coconut and chillies and stir till light golden. Add the onion and salt and cook for about 10 minutes till golden brown.

Now add the garlic, ginger, lime leaves, lime zest and juice and mix well. Add the beef and cook till brown.

Add the stock and coconut cream, bring to the boil and simmer till the liquid has reduced and thickened.

While the beef is simmering, make the parathas. Take the block of pastry out of the packet and cut into nine equal squares. Roll into balls, then roll out on a floured surface to about 15cm diameter. In a dry non-stick frying pan, fry each paratha on both sides till golden brown.

Before serving the rendang, crush the coriander and coconut with a pestle and mortar till you have a vibrant green garnish. Sprinkle on top of the rendang and serve with the parathas.

serves 4

prep 20 mins

cook 40 mins

tamarind chicken

Tamarind is a staple in my cooking and combined with chicken, it's pretty spectacular. It's tangy, sweet and spicy – all the good stuff! I like to serve with my squiggly potatoes, which are crispy and fun (even for grown-ups!) and give the perfect potatoey sponge to mop up any juices from the tamarind chicken.

For the squiggly potatoes

1kg potatoes, peeled and roughly chopped

oil, for greasing

1 teaspoon salt

1 tablespoon paprika

For the tamarind chicken

oil, for frying

7 spring onions, sliced in half on an angle

3 tablespoons vinegar

1 teaspoon sugar

4 chicken quarters

1 onion, chopped

3 cloves of garlic

2 teaspoons chilli powder

2 teaspoons curry powder

4 tablespoons tamarind paste

1 tablespoon fish sauce

1 tablespoon soy sauce

½ teaspoon salt

1 lemon, zest and juice

Preheat the oven to 200°C/fan 180°C and grease a baking tray with oil.

Start by making the squiggly potatoes. Pop the potatoes into a pan filled with water, bring to the boil and cook until tender. Drain, press through a ricer and lay across the baking tray. Mix the salt and paprika together, then sprinkle this over the potatoes.

Bake in the oven for 25–30 minutes, till crisp on top.

Meanwhile, make the tamarind chicken. Pour 2 tablespoons of oil into a large frying pan and get the oil hot. Add the spring onions quickly to fry fast in the oil. As soon as they are bubbling, charred and coloured (this should take about 2 minutes) take them out and pop onto a plate.

Mix the vinegar with the sugar and drizzle all over the spring onions.

Now add the chicken pieces in, skin-side down, and cook till browned all over. This should take about 5 minutes. Remove and set aside.

Add the onion and cook for 10 minutes till brown. Add the garlic and cook through, then add the chilli, curry powder, tamarind, fish sauce, soy sauce and salt. Mix until the spices are cooked through and the onion really melted. Add the lemon zest and juice.

Add the chicken back in, mix, cover and cook on a low heat for 45 minutes.

Take the chicken off the heat and before eating, add the pickled spring onions on top together with a nice slab of squiggly potato.

serves 4

prep 25 mins

cook 1 hr 5 mins

sweet-and-sour prawns

This isn't even about recreating a takeaway meal, because when I want the ease of ordering food, no amount of replicating at home will compete with the need to do nothing. So instead, this is for when you just know you want sweet-and-sour prawns! Packed with sweet veg, pineapple, cashews and crispy prawns, it's perfect with noodles.

For the prawns

100g cornflour

2 egg whites

1 teaspoon ground black pepper

½ teaspoon salt

2 tablespoons cold water

oil, for frying

300g raw king prawns

For the sauce

oil, for frying

50g cashews

3 cloves of garlic, sliced

1 red onion, cut into 3cm chunks

2 red peppers, cut into 3cm chunks

220g tin of pineapple, chopped into chunks

4 tablespoons ketchup

3 tablespoons vinegar

To serve

chopped fresh coriander

3 spring onions, chopped in long pieces

cooked noodles

Put the cornflour in a bowl with the egg whites, pepper, salt and water. Mix to a smooth paste.

Pour the oil into a frying pan so you have a thin layer of oil covering the base of the pan. Dip the prawns in the batter and fry over a high heat for 3–4 minutes until crispy and golden on both sides. You will need to do this in a few batches. Drain on kitchen paper.

Now wipe out the pan and pour in another drizzle of oil. Add the cashews and toast until golden. Add the slices of garlic and cook till crisp and brown.

Add the onion and pepper chunks and cook till just soft but still crunchy – this should only take 3–4 minutes. Now add the pineapple, ketchup and vinegar and mix through.

Toss in the prawns and mix through, then finish by mixing in the coriander and spring onions. Serve with noodles.

serves 4 | prep 15 mins | cook 20 mins

beignets with lemon curd

I first ate these while on my travels, though it was having seen them in the film *The Princess and the Frog*, dusted with copious amounts of icing sugar, which led me to them. As usual, I had to make my own version of these small, crisp, fried doughnuts, dusted in all the icing sugar and served with a warm lemon curd.

For the beignets

225g plain flour

1 teaspoon baking powder

50g melted butter

275ml boiling water

oil, for frying

icing sugar, for dusting

For the warm curd

2 lemons, zest and juice

100g caster sugar

50g butter

2 medium eggs

1 tablespoon cornflour

Mix the flour and baking powder together in a bowl. Tip in the melted butter, followed by the boiling water. Beat together briefly with an electric whisk until the dough is smooth and coming away from the edges.

Heat the oil to 180°C in a deep, heavy-bottomed saucepan or deep-fat fryer. Drop in walnut-size balls of the dough and fry in batches for 4–5 minutes until golden all over. Drain on kitchen paper and dust with icing sugar.

Meanwhile, make the warm curd by putting the lemon zest and juice, sugar, butter, eggs and cornflour in a small pan and mixing on a low heat till the mixture thickens. You know it is ready when the mixture coats the back of the spoon.

Serve the curd warm, with the beignets for dipping.

makes 30   prep 20 mins   cook 35 mins

lemon syllabub

The simplest of all recipes, this set-custard-slash-mousse pot is creamy, zesty and entirely foolproof. Using very few ingredients, the syllabub is infused with thyme and set with lemon juice. Simply serve with sponge fingers and a good cup of coffee.

150g raspberries

1 teaspoon rose extract

a sprig of fresh lemon thyme, leaves picked

300ml double cream

50g caster sugar

1 lemon, zest and juice

sponge fingers, to serve

Have four serving glasses or jam jars ready.

Mix the raspberries with the rose extract and lemon thyme leaves and mash a little to break up. Divide the mixture into the four glasses.

Add the cream and sugar to a mixing bowl and whip to soft peaks. Add the lemon zest and juice and fold through. Spoon on top of the raspberries. Ideally chill for an hour before serving, but you can eat it straight away!

Serve with sponge fingers.

serves
4

prep
15 mins
+1 hour
chilling

cook
no
cook

lemon drizzle swirls

Fresh cinnamon buns are just edible joy, all swirled up in your hands. These are like those but with lemon. It's a soft, sweet dough, baked with swirls of sugary lemon zest filling and topped with a thick creamy, lemony frosting.

For the dough

600g strong bread flour, plus extra for dusting

14g fast-action yeast

75g golden caster sugar

90g unsalted butter, softened

275ml lukewarm whole milk

1 teaspoon almond extract

1 medium egg

oil, for greasing the tin

For the filling

45g unsalted butter, softened

175g golden caster sugar

2 lemons, zest only

4 cardamom pods, seeds crushed to a fine powder or ½ tsp ground cardamom

a pinch of salt

For the frosting

110g unsalted butter, softened

250g full-fat cream cheese

5 tablespoons icing sugar

1 tablespoon vanilla bean paste

1 lemon, zest only

makes 12

prep 35 mins + rising

cook 20 mins

Start by making the dough. Put the flour, yeast and sugar in a mixing bowl or the bowl of a freestanding mixer. Mix well. Add the softened butter and using the tips of your fingers rub the butter in till there are no large lumps left. Create a well in the centre.

In a bowl or jug, whisk together the milk, almond extract and egg. Pour this into the dry mix. Attach the dough hook and mix. If there are still dry bits on the base, add a spoonful of water at a time till there are no dry bits of flour. As soon as it has come together, knead on high for 7 minutes.

Take out and shape into a neat ball, cover with cling film and leave in a warm place till it's doubled in size.

Make the filling by mixing the butter, sugar, lemon zest, cardamom and salt together and set aside.

Grease a 30 x 24cm brownie tin. Once the dough has doubled in size, dust the surface with flour and tip out. Roll out the dough to a 50 x 30cm rectangle, keeping the longer side closer to you.

Spoon the filling mixture onto the dough and spread all over using the back of a spoon. Roll from the long side like a swiss roll. Cut into 12 equal pieces. Place into the tray swirl-side up, 3 up, 4 across. Place them so they are just touching.

Grease a piece of cling film and cover. Leave in a warm place to prove again till the edges just touch.

Preheat the oven to 180°C/fan 160°C. Take the cling film off and bake for 20 minutes. Take out and leave to cool till just warm.

Make the frosting by putting the butter, cream cheese, icing sugar, vanilla bean paste and lemon zest in a bowl and mixing well. Generously spread all over. Tear and share . . . and enjoy.

orange blossom knots

These little bready knots are packed with zing. The simple sweet dough is flavoured with orange and they're served with a creamy posset of lemon and orange blossom. Tear, spread and devour!

For the dough

500g strong bread flour

7g fast-action yeast

2 teaspoons caster sugar

1 teaspoon salt

1 tablespoon butter, melted

1 orange, zest only

300ml warm water

For the posset

1 egg, lightly beaten

80ml golden syrup, warmed to make runnier

40g pistachios, roughly chopped

For the glaze

600ml double cream

200g caster sugar

3 lemons, zest plus 75ml juice

1 teaspoon orange blossom water

Start by making the knots. Put the flour in a bowl with the yeast and sugar on one side and the salt on the other side. Drizzle in the melted butter and mix, then add the orange zest and mix.

Make a well in the centre and pour in the warm water. Bring the dough together. Knead on the work surface or with a dough hook in a freestanding mixer for 6 minutes on high, till the dough is stretchy and smooth. Put in a bowl, cover and leave in a warm place to double in size.

Make the posset by putting the cream in a saucepan. Mix the sugar in, turn on the heat and begin to simmer the mixture, leaving it to bubble away for 1 minute. Take off the heat and leave for just a few minutes. Add the zest and juice and mix well. It should begin to thicken.

Pour into nine small ramekins or jam jars and leave to set in the fridge. Line two baking trays with paper.

Once the dough has doubled in size, knock out the air and divide into nine balls. Roll each ball into a 25cm sausage and knot, making sure the seam is always on the base. Pop onto the tray, cover with greased cling film and leave to double in size again.

Preheat the oven to 180°C/fan 160°C. Brush each knot with egg and bake for 18–20 minutes.

As soon as they are out, leave for 10 minutes on the tray, then brush all over with the warmed golden syrup and sprinkle over the pistachios. They are then ready to be eaten with the posset.

recipe photographs over page ▶

serves
9

prep
30 mins + risisng

cook
25 mins

cranberry crumble bars

I have been making these bars since I first started baking and especially since having children, as they are so easy to make and pack away for snacks and treats. It's a straightforward dough recipe, with a tart cranberry filling and the same dough crumbled on top. Simple to make and simpler to eat, there is no such thing as eating just one bar!

For the batter

75g plain flour

200g caster sugar

1 teaspoon baking powder

a pinch of salt

230g unsalted butter, plus extra for greasing the tin

1 medium egg

60ml whole milk

2 teaspoons vanilla extract

150g frozen cranberries

10g caster sugar

1 tablespoon cornflour

1 lime, zest and juice

For the icing

120g icing sugar

2 tablespoons lime juice

Start by greasing and lining a 23cm square tin and preheating the oven to 190°C/fan 170°C.

Put the flour in a bowl with the caster sugar, baking powder and salt. Mix together. Add the butter and crumble in using your fingers until there are no lumps.

Make a well in the centre, pour the egg, milk and vanilla into it and bring the dough together.

Take a third of the dough and set aside. Take the remaining two-thirds of the dough and push into the base of the tin till compact.

To make the filling, mix the cranberries, caster sugar, cornflour, lime zest and juice together in a bowl, then pour over the biscuit base. Now take the rest of the biscuit base mix and crumble all over the cranberries. Bake for 45–50 minutes.

Take out and leave to cool in the tin, then remove from the tin. Mix the icing sugar and lime juice together, drizzle the icing over and cut into squares to serve.

makes 20 · prep 25 mins · cook 50 mins

EARTHY

grits with spinach and mushroom

I had never eaten grits till I was filming out in the USA, in Louisiana, when during a rushed morning of work I was handed a tall, hot, Styrofoam cup with a lid on top. Hungry and tired, I uncovered delicious cooked mushrooms and tofu all served on a cup full of grits. That was my kind of breakfast, so I have recreated it here, topped with flavour-packed mushrooms and tofu, plus some zingy kimchi. Not exactly as I remember it on my travels, but certainly a yummy variation of a breakfast that will stay with me forever.

100g polenta

4 portobello mushrooms (300g)

700ml water

1 vegetable stock cube

50ml extra-virgin olive oil

Spinach and mushroom topping

4 tablespoons extra-virgin olive oil, plus extra for drizzling

a small handful of spinach

2 cloves of garlic, crushed

¼ teaspoon ground turmeric

280g firm tofu, cut into 1cm cubes

½ teaspoon salt

10 cherry tomatoes, halved

4 tablespoons kimchi

Take a medium to large saucepan that has a lid. Pour the polenta into the base and on a high heat, dry-fry it to really enhance and extract the flavour of the corn. Keep mixing and stirring till you have a mixture that is speckled. If you are unsure about the colour or feel it isn't toasting, look at your jar or packet of polenta to see the difference and you will see, it definitely is. This should only take 4–5 minutes. Take off the heat and pour into a bowl.

Now on to making the grits. Start with the mushroom gills – these are the dark underside of the mushrooms that quite literally look like gills. Remove the mushroom stalks and cube them for the topping, then scrape the gills out using a teaspoon (this will add an intense earthy flavour and colour to the finished grits). Add the gills to the same pan you used to toast the polenta.

Add the water to the pan along with the crumbled stock cube and bring to the boil. As soon as it comes up to a boil, turn the heat to medium and then shoot in the polenta. Be ready to whisk instantly, and keep whisking till the mixture is quite thick. As soon as it is, add the oil and give it a really vigorous whisk, lower the heat to your lowest setting and pop the lid on, leaving a small crack to allow steam to escape (this will make it cook in half the time). Steam for 10 minutes.

method continued over page ▶

serves 4

prep 20 mins

cook 35 mins

Now on to our fast-delicious topping. Have a small plate at the ready, lined with paper, to scoop our spinach onto. Pour the olive oil into a non-stick frying pan and turn up the heat till the pan of oil is smoking. Sprinkle the spinach in (be careful as the oil will spit as you do this) in an even layer and let the spinach really crisp up. This should literally only take a few seconds. As soon as they crisp up, remove the pan from the heat and scoop up the spinach onto the plate using a slotted spoon. Lightly season and keep the spinach crisp.

Put the same pan back onto a medium heat and add the crushed garlic and turmeric, cooking gently for a few seconds till just golden. Add the tofu and cook till the tofu is toasty in colour and golden.

Season, add the diced mushrooms and stir till the mushrooms are soft. To finish, add the cherry tomatoes and mix through to simply heat up. Take off the heat. Add the kimchi and mix through.

To serve, take the grits off the heat. If the mixture feels a little stiff to stir, add a few splashes of hot water to loosen it. Spread the grits all over a platter. Place the spinach, cooked tofu and mushrooms on top and drizzle over any juices that are left over in the bottom of the pan. Drizzle over a little olive oil to serve.

lentil hummus

Hummus is the pacifier of hunger, the calmer of children, something to tide you over till the real hole-filling food is served. But it doesn't have to always be that way. It can be the main event if you make it a little bit different, such as this hummus, which is made with tinned lentils, enhanced by nutmeg and sweetened with a touch of maple syrup. This is the simplest recipe ever and a great alternative to chickpea hummus.

400g tin of lentils, drained

1 teaspoon ground nutmeg

100g tahini

5 tablespoons olive oil

2 cloves of garlic

1 lemon, zest and juice

1 tablespoon maple syrup

a large pinch of sea salt

To serve

a drizzle of olive oil

a drizzle of maple syrup

a small handful of fresh parsley, roughly chopped

a sprinkling of grated nutmeg

Put all the lentils except for 1 tablespoon (set this aside for later) in a food processor and whizz them till they become smoother.

Now add everything else – the nutmeg, tahini, oil, garlic, lemon zest and juice, maple syrup and salt – and whizz till you have a smooth paste. Check the seasoning, adding more salt if needed.

Transfer onto a plate and swirl into a thin layer. To finish, add the reserved lentils into the centre.

Drizzle over the oil and then the maple syrup. Sprinkle over the parsley and lastly grate the nutmeg.

As a lunch, I love serving this with toasted chopped pitta, a few raw mangetouts and chopped carrots.

serves 4–6   prep 15 mins   cook no cook

toast with anchovy and beetroot butter

To be totally honest, I don't need new ways of eating butter. I can eat it as it is, with some salt, and be quite happy with no human contact – just bread, butter and my own company. However, there are some really cool ways of jazzing up butter and this is one of my faves, with salty anchovies, earthy cumin and sweet bright beetroot! This is simple and delicious and easy to make.

250g cooked beetroot, vacuum-sealed packet variety

100g unsalted butter, softened

15 anchovy fillets

1 teaspoon ground cumin, plus an extra pinch

To serve

4 slices of sourdough bread

olive oil, for the bread and eggs

2 avocados, sliced, with a squeeze of lime juice for flavour and to stop browning

4 eggs

Roughly chop the beetroot, pat dry in paper towels to remove any moisture and add to a food processor. Whizz till no longer in large chunks.

Add the butter, anchovies and ground cumin and whizz till you have a smooth paste. The butter is ready.

To serve, I like to lightly oil both sides of the sourdough and pan-fry till just charred. Remove, spread with the butter, and add the sliced avocado on top.

Using the same pan, heat a few tablespoons of oil till smoking hot, sprinkle in a decent pinch of ground cumin, crack in the eggs and fry till the whites are cooked, the yolk is runny and the edges are frilly.

Add the eggs on top of the avocado and drizzle over the remainder of the cumin oil.

If you have any butter left over, it makes for a great sauce to coat freshly cooked pasta or spaghetti.

serves 4 / prep 5 mins / cook 5 mins

sage and onion gnocchi

Gnocchi need not be out of a packet, and nor does it have to be tricky to make. There are simple ways of doing it, such as this recipe, which uses instant mashed potatoes and tinned mushrooms to create a delicious version. The earthiness of the mushrooms and yeast, and the fragrance of the sage, make this a winning, and little bit extraordinary, dinner.

For the gnocchi

285g tin of button mushrooms

2 teaspoons yeast extract

109g packet of instant mash potato flakes

100g plain flour, plus extra for dusting

For the sage and onion sauce

2 tablespoons unsalted butter

2 onions, thinly sliced

10 fresh sage leaves

1 vegetable stock cube

200g crème fraîche

1 packet of fresh chives (30g), roughly chopped

a squeeze of lemon juice

Pop the contents of the mushroom tin, all of it, into a pan along with the yeast extract and bring the whole thing to a boil. As soon as it has boiled, stir it to make sure that the yeast extract has dissolved. Cool a little and pop into a blender to create a smooth purée.

Add the potato flakes and flour to a bowl and mix well till combined. Make a well in the centre and add the hot mushroom liquid to it, using a palette knife to bring it together as much as you can, then get your hands in and get mixing till you have a smooth dough ball.

Roll the dough into a thick sausage and divide equally into four pieces. Lightly flour the surface and roll each piece out to about a 30cm sausage. Then, using a knife, cut each sausage into 16 equal pieces. Flour a tray and, using the back of a fork, indent each gnocchi piece. Do this by holding the fork, popping the dough piece onto the back of the fork and using the side of your thumb to push the gnocchi down gently along the spokes of the fork whilst moving your finger away from you and you should have indentations.

Bring a medium pan of salted water to the boil and then add the gnocchi gently. You want to do this in three batches. As soon as you put the first third in, they will sink, then as soon as they rise to the top, they are cooked (about 3–4 minutes per batch). Use a slotted spoon to remove, drain and pop back onto the tray. Do this to the rest until they are all cooked.

Put a large non-stick frying pan onto a heat with the butter, bring to a high heat and cook the butter till brown. Add the onion slices and cook over the high heat for 3–4 minutes until golden and scorched in places. Lower the heat.

Add the sage leaves and allow to just crisp up, then add the gnocchi and leave on a medium to high heat so the gnocchi pieces char and get some of that golden colour. Crumble in the stock cube and stir through.

Add the chives to a jug with 2 tablespoons of the crème fraîche and the lemon juice and blend with a stick blender. Add the rest of the crème fraîche and mix with a spoon.

Take the gnocchi off the heat and drizzle over the crème fraîche. Serve any extra sauce in a bowl alongside.

recipe photographs over page ▶

serves
4

prep
30 mins

cook
25 mins

thirty-clove garlic chicken with roti jalla

Garlic doesn't scare me, but even just writing 30 cloves made me wonder whether you will think it's too much! But seriously, you have to trust me when I say whole garlic cooked gently into a rich sauce is a thing of utter beauty. This chicken is smoky, rich and gently garlicky, and is served with netted pancakes that are fun to make.

For the chicken

30 cloves of garlic (approx. 3 bulbs), unpeeled

500ml water

2 onions, peeled and quartered (210g)

1½ teaspoons fine salt

1 tablespoon smoked paprika

1 tablespoon garam masala

1½ tablespoons tomato purée

3 tablespoons vegetable oil

1 lemon, halved

1.2kg chicken, quartered, on the bone, skin removed and flesh scored

50g black olives, thinly sliced

Start by adding the cloves of garlic to a small pan with the water. Pop onto the stove on a high heat and as soon as the water comes to a boil, lower the heat to medium and leave to simmer away for 10 minutes.

Add the onion quarters, salt, paprika, garam masala and tomato purée to a food processor or blender.

Drain the garlic cloves into a colander, making sure to reserve the boiling liquid into a separate bowl. Save the garlic cloves for later. Add the cooking water to the processor and whizz to a smooth paste.

Add the oil to a large flat casserole dish that has a lid. Add the two lemon halves to the pan and whack the heat up to high. This will gently release flavour into the oil.

Take the onion mixture over to the pan. Remove the lemon halves. Pour the onion mixture in, squeeze all the juice out of the lemon halves and discard the flesh.

Take the garlic cloves and remove any bits of skin that have not already fallen off. Add the garlic into the pan and cook the mixture with the lid off to dry out on a medium to high heat for 7 minutes or until the mixture is dry and there are no watery bits left in the pan.

Add the chicken, stir through the mixture, cover and leave on a medium heat for 25 minutes. Be sure to give the whole thing a mix and turn the chicken onto the other side about halfway through cooking. If the sauce starts to catch, add a little water to the pan.

method, ingredients and recipe photo continued over page ▶

For the roti jalla

200g chickpea flour, sifted

1 teaspoon salt

1 teaspoon onion seeds

4 medium eggs

250ml whole milk

2 tablespoons oil, plus extra for greasing the pan

Meanwhile, make the roti batter by adding the sifted chickpea flour to a bowl with the salt and onion seeds and whisking through. Add the eggs, milk and oil and whisk till you have a smooth batter.

Take a 24cm pancake pan and pop onto a high heat. Brush lightly with oil and then take tablespoons of the pancake mixture and drizzle all over the pan to make a lacy pancake. You will get larger clumps and smaller threads, which will mean all sorts of textures and shapes. You will need about 3–4 tablespoons of the mixture for each pancake. As soon as they hit the pan, they take about 30–45 seconds to cook. They are ready to flip over when the top has formed bubbles and they look dry on the surface. Turn out onto a plate and keep going till you have used up all the batter.

Once the chicken is cooked, take off the heat, add the sliced olives and stir through. Move the chicken pieces around to create gaps in which to place the roti jalla. Pinch together a couple of the pancakes, bundle them up and pop them into the gaps.

Serve in the centre of the table and spoon up.

serves
4
(16 roti jalla)

prep
15 mins

cook
40 mins

mixed bean lasagne

I have tried, tested and reimagined so many different types of lasagne, but I especially love this simple cheaty bean version. Tinned beans take half the time to cook than ones from scratch, and the white sauce is just cottage cheese and eggs, making this perfect for when you simply want lasagne and you want it now!

For the beans

2 tablespoons cumin seeds

2 tablespoons coriander seeds

5 tablespoons vegetable oil

2 tablespoons garlic paste

3 x 400g tins of mixed beans, drained and rinsed

1 teaspoon salt

2 tablespoons Worcestershire sauce

2 x 400g tins of chopped tomatoes

1 packet of fresh flat-leaf parsley (30g)

For the white sauce

2 medium eggs, beaten

600g cottage cheese

a pinch of salt

To assemble

9 lasagne sheets

100g smoked hard cheese, grated

serves 6 · prep 20 mins · cook 1hr 25 mins

Start by crushing the cumin and coriander seeds – not to a fine dust, but not whole either, ground so they are broken down.

Put the spices in a saucepan and pop onto a medium to high heat. Start mixing the spices, stirring all the time, till they are aromatic and lightly toasted – this should only take a few minutes.

Add the oil and allow the spices to sizzle. Add the garlic paste and cook till golden. Put half a tin of the drained beans into a bowl and add the rest of them to the pan with the spices. Gently stir through.

Add the salt, Worcestershire sauce and chopped tomatoes, then mix and leave on a medium heat to simmer for 10 minutes.

Crush the beans that you kept behind using the back of a fork, making sure to burst every bean – the starch in the beans will help to thicken the sauce. We are not looking for a smooth paste, just crushed beans. Pop those straight in and simmer for another 10 minutes, then finely chop the parsley and stir it through to combine.

Meanwhile, preheat the oven to 180°C/fan 160°C and have a 30 x 22cm lasagne dish ready.

Make the white sauce by adding the eggs, cottage cheese and salt to a bowl and mixing through.

Add half the bean mixture into the base of the dish. Then layer 4 and ½ of the lasagne sheets, so the beans are covered in an even layer without any overlap.

Add half the white sauce all over the sheets. Now repeat using the bean mix, then the sheets, then the sauce again. Add the cheese on top and bake in the oven for 1 hour. Serve with peas or salad.

lamb mole with lemon rice

On a trip away for work, in a community where Mexican food is some of the best in the world, we stopped for an unassuming buffet lunch where mole was served, of all varieties, some with veg, others with chicken and meats, all in that rich, dark sauce. I happened to not be very hungry that day but I still regret not eating my full plate as it was the kind of food you know takes care and attention to make. So, this is my version of mole: lamb cooked in a rich cocoa-infused sauce, my recreation of that memory to make up for the half-eaten meal, served with a zingy lemon rice.

For the pickled onions

2 small red onions, thinly sliced into rings

3 tablespoons vinegar

For the mole

2 tablespoons vegetable oil

2 tablespoons dried chilli flakes

50g crispy fried onions

3 tablespoons garlic powder

1 tablespoon smoked paprika

1 tablespoon salt

2 tablespoons cocoa powder

Start by making the pickled onions. Add the vinegar to the onions, mix and leave to soften while you get on with the rest of the dish.

To make the sauce, put the chilli, onions, garlic, paprika, salt, cocoa, cinnamon, peanut butter, tomatoes, dates and lemon juice in a food processer. Fill the emptied tin of tomatoes with water and add that to the processor too. Blitz to a smooth paste.

Pour the oil into a large non-stick pan. As soon as the oil is hot, add the lamb and cook until browned all over.

Add the sauce and cook on a high heat for 10 minutes, stirring all the time, and then reduce to medium and cook for 30 minutes till the sauce has thickened and the colour has deepened. You will know that the spices are cooked when the oil has risen to the top. If the sauce catches, add a small splash of water.

While it cooks, get on to the rice. Heat the oil in a small non-stick saucepan. Once hot, add the rind of the lemon and allow a few seconds for the oil to release.

serves 4

prep 15 mins

cook 40 mins

1 teaspoon ground
cinnamon

4 tablespoons smooth
peanut butter (about 75g)

400g tin of chopped
tomatoes

50g pitted dates

1 lemon, rind removed
for the rice, juice for the
sauce

900g diced lamb,

**For the
lemon rice**

5 tablespoons oil

500g basmati rice

a pinch of salt

1 litre boiling water

Add the rice straight in and fry for a few minutes, till it looks whiter.
Sprinkle in the salt, stir through, then pour in the hot water. Keep
stirring and cooking on a high heat till the water has really thickened.

As soon as the water is thick and really reduced and the rice just
starts catching the bottom of the pan, turn the heat right down,
cover and steam for 10 minutes on the lowest heat.

Once the mole is cooked, fluff up the rice and serve topped with the
mole and pickled onions.

coronation aubergine

Aubergines often feature as a side dish when served at a table for dinner, but not here. We are taking this delicious aubergine, coating it with flavour, frying till tender and then drizzling over the simplest coronation dressing. It's like dinner at my mum's collided with my lunches at school to create this beauty.

For the aubergine

225ml olive oil

3 cloves of garlic, minced

1 small onion, grated

1 teaspoon paprika

1 teaspoon salt

2 large aubergines, sliced into 1cm thick slices (about 600g)

For the dressing

200g Greek yoghurt

2 teaspoons curry powder

2 cloves of garlic, minced

½ teaspoon salt

2 tablespoons mango chutney, finely chopped

2 tablespoons whole milk

To serve

a small handful of crispy fried onions

a small handful of raisins

a small handful of fresh coriander, thinly sliced

Start by putting the oil in a bowl with the minced garlic, onion, paprika and salt. Mix really well and set aside with a pastry brush.

Pop the aubergines onto a tray (they can overlap, that is fine). Take the oil mixture and brush the aubergine slices generously with the oil on both sides till you have finished all the mixture. Set aside.

Put one large or two small (if you have them) griddle pan(s) onto a medium heat (these are great on the barbecue, too, FYI).

Griddle in batches on both sides. They take approx. 2 minutes on each side. You will know they are ready when the flesh looks saturated, less spongy and softer. Pop onto a plate, overlapping, ready to serve.

Make the dressing by combining the yoghurt, curry powder, garlic, salt and mango chutney and giving it all a really good mix. Add a few tablespoons of whole milk to loosen the mixture just a little.

Drizzle the dressing all over the top of the aubergine, saving the rest to serve on the side. Sprinkle with fried onions, raisins and coriander to serve.

serves 4–6 | prep 25 mins | cook 20 mins

apple and olive oil cake

This cake is dense and sweet, with tartness and an unexpected bite from the apple sauce, while the olive oil makes it moist and fragrant. The cake is not only vegan, it's also gluten free – but most of all, it's delicious.

For the cake

180ml extra-virgin olive oil

220g caster sugar

2 teaspoons baking powder

180g chunky apple sauce

200g ground almonds, sifted

200g gluten-free plain flour, sifted

For the syrup

250ml apple juice

100g caster sugar

1 teaspoon mixed spice

For the olive oil icing

80ml extra-virgin olive oil

80g icing sugar, sifted

Start by lining and greasing a 20cm deep cake tin and preheating the oven to 200°C/fan 180°C.

Pour the oil and sugar into a bowl and whisk together for 2 minutes till the mixture is combined and pale. Put the baking powder and apple sauce into a smaller bowl and mix together. Add to the oil-sugar mix and whizz together till well combined.

Now add the ground almonds and plain flour, then fold through till everything is well combined. You should have a dense, grainy batter. Spoon into the lined cake tin, smooth with the back of a spoon and bake for 30 minutes.

Make the syrup by putting the apple juice and sugar into a pan. Bring to the boil and then leave to simmer for 10 minutes, till reduced by half. Take off the heat, add the mixed spice and stir through.

After 30 minutes, reduce the oven temperature to 180°C/fan 160°C and pop a sheet of foil on top of the cake tin to stop the top from browning too much. Bake for another 25 minutes.

As soon as the cake comes out of the oven, poke holes into it and pour the syrup mixture all over. Leave to cool completely in the tin.

Meanwhile, make the icing by putting the oil and icing sugar in a jug and blitzing until thick and well combined (or blend with a stick blender).

As soon as the cake is cooled, remove it from the tin, add the icing right on top and it's ready to eat. This will keep in the fridge for 4 days.

serves 4 prep 15 mins cook 1 hour

demerara and Earl Grey tray bake

Some of the most delicious cakes need only the simplest ingredients. This is one of those cakes, which relies almost entirely on ingredients from your store cupboard. It involves a light joconde sponge, made with toasted ground almonds and meringue, and a strong Earl Grey syrup, which gets brushed over the sponge to make it sticky. It's finally filled and topped with a smooth Earl Grey crème for a subtle but beautiful layered tray bake.

For the syrup

125ml boiling water

6 Earl Grey tea bags

40g caster sugar

For the cake

25g demerara sugar

100g ground almonds

3 medium egg whites (save the yolks for the crème)

150g golden caster sugar

100g icing sugar

For the crème

3 medium eggs

30g plain flour, sifted

25g unsalted butter, melted, plus extra for greasing the tin

3 medium egg yolks

75g caster sugar

225g unsalted butter, softened to room temperature

To make the syrup, pour the boiling water over the tea bags in a jug and leave to infuse for 10 minutes.

For the cake, preheat the oven to 200°C/fan 180°C and grease and line a 30 x 20cm swiss roll tin. Sprinkle the demerara sugar in an even layer over the base of the tin and set aside.

Toast the ground almonds in a dry non-stick pan on a high heat, stirring all the time, till the almonds become golden and speckled in places. You should really be able to smell the almonds – this will take no more than 3 minutes. Pop onto a plate to cool completely.

Now, start the cake mixture by putting the egg whites in a clean bowl and whisking with an electric whisk. As soon as they start to get foamy, add the caster sugar one spoonful at a time, till you have used it all and you have a smooth, glossy and very shiny meringue mix.

Take the beaters out and set the bowl aside. Put the cooled almonds, icing sugar and whole eggs in another bowl and, using the same beaters, whisk till the mixture is light and fluffy. This can take from 5–10 minutes.

As soon as it is ready, add the flour and melted butter and, using a spatula, fold through till you have a thick cake batter.

Take a third of the meringue mixture and mix vigorously into the cake batter to loosen. Now add the next third and fold through till you have no more white meringue lumps. Do the same with the last third, till you have a smooth cake batter.

Pour into the prepared tin and bake for 10 minutes until golden.

Meanwhile, take the Earl Grey mix and squeeze the tea bags of all their liquid. Take 3 tablespoons of the liquid, reserving the rest for the crème, and put in a small bowl along with the 40g of sugar and mix together for an Earl Grey-infused syrup.

Once baked, leave the cake to cool completely in the tin. While it is still hot, brush all over with the syrup until the cake is completely drenched. Take it out of the tin and cut in half vertically so that you have two rectangles.

Make the crème by putting the egg yolks in a bowl (or freestanding mixer) and whisking. The colour will become just a little lighter and the mixture will have a little volume.

Meanwhile, add the sugar to a pan along with 3 tablespoons of the reserved Earl Grey tea mixture. Bring to a boil on a high heat, until the mixture comes to 110°C. This will take less than a minute.

Back to the egg yolks. Begin beating them again with the whisk to make sure the mixture is always moving, then slowly pour in the sugar mixture while whisking until it is all well combined. Take big pinches of the butter, or use a teaspoon, and add to the egg mixture, making sure to whisk well after each addition. Do this till you have used up all your butter. The mix should be velvety smooth. Leave to firm up in the fridge for 20 minutes.

Add half the crème to one rectangle and pop the other rectangle on top. With the rest of the crème, you can either pipe or dollop over the top. I like to dollop and spread, then just simply run the curved part of a teaspoon over to create ripples.

Cut into eight pieces and make a hot cup of Earl Grey to go with it! Leftovers will keep in the fridge for 2 days.

recipe photographs over page ▶

serves
8

prep
45 mins

cook
15 mins

treacle and prune tart

The simplicity and no-waste nature of this tart is what really makes me smile. It's a simple pastry case scented with ground star anise, filled with a deep treacle cake filling and dotted with juicy prunes. The spare pastry is baked and crumbled on top to encase this delicate tart with more of that subtle sweet anise and then drizzled with golden syrup.

For the tart

150g unsalted butter, cubed and left in the freezer

300g plain flour, plus extra for dusting

a pinch of salt

1 teaspoon ground star anise

7 tablespoons cold water (you may need more or less)

For the filling

50g treacle

50g golden syrup

2 medium eggs

100g unsalted butter, melted

200g self-raising flour

100g prunes, halved

For the topping

25g demerara sugar

3 tablespoons golden syrup

½ teaspoon ground star anise

Start by having a 10 inch (25cm) fluted loose-bottomed tart tin at the ready. This pastry is best suited to being made in a food processor, but if you are making it by hand skip the part where you put the cubes of butter in the freezer, it will just make it a little easier.

Add the butter, flour, salt and anise to the processor and blitz till the mixture is a coarse breadcrumb texture.

Add 5 tablespoons of water to begin with and blitz till it just starts to come together. If it does not come together, add another spoon until the mixture clumps together.

Take out of the processer and just bring the dough together. Roll out to about 5mm thick on a floured surface, enough to cover the base and sides of the tart tin and a little more.

Pick up the pastry using the rolling pin and line the base and sides with overhanging pastry. Be sure to tease the pastry into the fluted edge. Using a sharp knife, cut away the excess. Pop the pastry-lined tin into the freezer for 10 minutes until firm and bring the excess pastry together.

Preheat the oven to 200°C/fan 180°C and pop a tray on to the middle shelf of the oven.

Take the excess pastry and roll out to about 5mm thick. Pop onto a baking tray, sprinkle over the demerara sugar and push right in.

Take the tart shell out of the freezer and use a fork to pierce holes into the base of the pastry. Line with scrunched-up baking paper, add baking beads or dry rice/lentils and encourage into the edges. Pop the tart tin onto the hot baking tray and pop the tray with the excess pastry directly below.

Bake for 20 minutes. Take out the excess pastry and put to one side to cool. Take out the tart shell, remove the paper and beads/lentils/rice then pop the tart shell back in for another 10 minutes until light golden all over. Take out the shell and leave to cool.

Make the filling by adding the treacle, syrup and eggs to a bowl and whisk till the mixture is light and fluffy and lighter in colour. Add the butter and whisk through.

Add the self-raising flour and fold the flour through till mixed evenly. Pour the mixture into the pastry shell. Dot the prunes all over and roughly crumble the leftover pastry on top. Bake for 25 minutes.

Leave to cool in the tin till completely cold and remove. Before serving, drizzle over the sweet golden syrup, mixed with anise as a final flourish.

serves
6–8

prep
30 mins
+ cooling

cook
55
mins

wheat biscuit balls

I only started making these as a way of using up wheat biscuits to create something sweet with extra fibre, and what I didn't expect was for them to be quite so yummy. These are sticky with apricots, earthy from the crushed wheat biscuits, scented slightly with cardamom and delicious with every bite. Adorned with icing sugar and pistachios, they are just perfect for something quick and sweet.

250g dried apricots, soaked in 500ml boiling water

12 wheat biscuits

10 cardamom pods, seeds removed

4 tablespoons coconut oil

4 tablespoons golden syrup

To coat

100g pistachios

50g icing sugar

These are super simple to make. Be sure to soak your apricots first. Leave till the water is just warm.

Drain and pop to one side.

Add the wheat biscuits to a food processor and blitz to a fine crumb. Take the cardamom seeds and crush in a pestle and mortar and then add to the processor.

Add the drained apricots and whizz till well combined and the mixture begins to clump. Add the coconut oil and the golden syrup and whizz till it really begins to come together.

Take a small handful of the mixture (about 20g) and roll tight into a ball. Pop onto a tray and do the same to each one.

Blend the pistachios to a fine powder and mix with the icing sugar. Now take each ball and roll generously in the pistachio sugar to coat. Keep in the fridge for up to 5 days.

makes
36
small
balls

prep
5
mins

cook
no
cook

FRUITY

pineapple upside-down pancakes

Pancakes are a real thing in our house – we have them for breakfast every Saturday morning. If I dare suggest otherwise, the kids give me this look that says, 'What kind of monster are you?' So, to avoid that death stare and, of course, make them happy, we have pancakes. It doesn't even matter who makes them as long as someone does. We particularly love these ones which are topped with a pineapple ring and finished with a glacé cherry.

250g plain flour

1 teaspoon baking powder

½ teaspoon salt

3 tablespoons caster sugar

2 medium eggs

170ml whole milk

2 tablespoons oil, plus extra for greasing

435g tin of pineapple rings, drained

8 glacé cherries

6 teaspoons caster sugar

yoghurt, to serve

Start by making the batter. Put the flour, baking powder, salt and sugar in a mixing bowl then stir to combine.

Make a well in the centre and add the eggs and milk together with the oil. Whisk till you have a smooth batter.

Place a large non-stick pan on a medium heat with a small amount of oil.

Spoon 3 tablespoons of the batter into the pan and add a ring of pineapple and a glacé cherry in the centre. There should be space to cook two to three pancakes at a time.

Cook till the top looks dry and bubbles have appeared on the surface. This should take 3–4 minutes.

Add a sprinkling of sugar, turn over and cook for a few minutes till browned, pressing the edges of the pancakes down so they make contact with the pan.

Remove from the pan and repeat until you have finished the batter. Serve with yoghurt and a drizzle of honey, if you like.

serves 4

prep 15 mins

cook 25 mins

fruit cheesecake salad

This is the kind of fun breakfast I like to make when we have had pancakes every Saturday for all 52 weeks of the year. A colourful fruit salad topped onto toasted buttered croissants and served with my quick vanilla cream cheese sauce, it has all the flavours of a cheesecake, but for breakfast instead.

420g tin of sliced peaches, drained

300g frozen blackberries

225g strawberries, quartered

100g dried cranberries

100g pistachios, roughly chopped

250g full-fat cream cheese

1 tablespoon vanilla bean paste

3 tablespoons maple syrup

6 large croissants, halved

30g salted butter, melted

Start by putting the peaches, blackberries, strawberries, cranberries and pistachios in a bowl. Mix well.

Mix the cream cheese, vanilla and maple syrup in a separate bowl until smooth.

Cut or rip open the croissants lengthways and brush the insides with melted butter.

Pop a large non-stick pan on the heat, add the croissants, butter-side down, and toast for 1–2 minutes till golden. Do this till you have finished all of them.

Pop on a platter and add the fruit salad into the centre of the croissants. Spoon over the cream cheese filling and it is ready to eat.

serves
6

prep
15 mins

cook
5 mins

squash, saffron and grapefruit soup

With kids and colds being best mates, soups are a must in our house, and we like to find ways of reinventing them so they are just a little bit different, if not for them, then at least for me! This squash is cooked and zinged up with grapefruit. I like to crisp up the seeds and use them as a garnish for the top.

4 tablespoons oil

1kg squash, peeled and chopped into small cubes (save the seeds)

2 teaspoons salt

1 teaspoon mango powder

7–8cm ginger, peeled and minced

a small pinch of saffron strands

750ml hot water

1 grapefruit, all the juice but only ½ the zest

To serve

soured cream

olive oil

Pour the oil into a large saucepan. As soon as the oil is hot, add the squash seeds. When the seeds are crisp and brown, pop onto a plate with kitchen paper using a slotted spoon. Sprinkle over the salt and mango powder.

To the same oil, add the ginger and cook for a minute. Add the saffron and stir through.

Now add the squash and fry for a few minutes. As soon as the squash has some colour, pour in the water and grapefruit juice and add the zest. Mix and leave to boil. As soon as it has boiled, simmer on medium heat for 20 minutes till the squash has cooked right through.

Take off the heat and use a stick blender to make smooth.

Serve the soup with a dollop of soured cream, some squash seeds and a drizzle of olive oil.

serves 4   prep 15 mins   cook 40 mins

mango noodle salad

If I am going to have a salad it has to be packed with flavour, *all* the flavour! This is a delicious cold noodle salad, mixed with crisped shredded chicken, dressed in a sweet, spicy, sour, fruity mango dressing and topped with a whole lot of freshness and colour from crunchy peppers and spring onions.

225g rice vermicelli noodles

3 tablespoons oil

2 cooked chicken breasts (210g), shredded

2 cloves of garlic, thinly sliced

1 mango, peeled and cubed

a small handful of fresh coriander

2 red chillies

1 teaspoon salt

1 lemon, zest and juice

salt and ground black pepper

To serve

3 spring onions, thinly sliced into strips

a small handful of fresh coriander, sliced

1 red pepper, thinly sliced

1 yellow pepper, thinly sliced

Start by putting the noodles in a bowl and adding boiling water to it till the noodles are submerged. Leave according to the instructions on the packet. Drain into a colander and run under cold water until totally cold, then put in a large bowl.

Now pop a non-stick frying pan onto the hob and pour in the oil. Heat the oil on high, add the shredded chicken in an even layer and fry. As soon as it is crisp on the base, turn around in bits and crisp up the other side. Transfer onto a plate and lightly season.

To the same pan add the garlic and cook till very golden brown. As soon as it is, use a slotted spoon and add the garlic to a food processor. Now add the mango, coriander, chillies, salt, lemon zest and juice to the food processor and blend to a smooth sauce. Add the sauce to the noodles.

Before serving, add the spring onion, coriander, both the red and yellow peppers and toss through. Stir in the chicken and it's ready to serve and enjoy.

recipe photographs over page ▶

serves 6

prep 25 mins

cook 10 mins

Thai cucumber salad

The first time I tasted a papaya salad I was out in Thailand, and I can't imagine anything ever beating that disco that was happening in my mouth. Papaya is not so easy to come by here in the UK, and when I do see it, I often have to walk right on by as it can be pricey. But I wasn't going to let an overpriced papaya get in the way of my delicious salad, so I've created my version using the humble cucumber. Crunchy, strong and aromatic: same disco, different crowd!

100g green beans

2 cucumbers

2 tomatoes

1 large carrot

1 red onion

150g cooked prawns

60g roasted salted peanuts, plus 25g extra for serving

For the sauce

2–4 bird's eye chillies

3 cloves of garlic

1 tablespoon brown sugar

2 limes, juice only

3 tablespoons fish sauce

Start by cutting the green beans into 2–3cm pieces. Blanch in hot water for 4 minutes. Drain, run under cold water and leave to cool.

Peel the cucumbers and remove the central watery, seedy bit. Slice into thin strips. Pop into a large bowl. Halve the tomatoes and scoop out the centre. Slice very thin and pop into the bowl.

Peel and thinly slice the carrot into strips, same as the cucumber, and add to the bowl. Take the red onion, thinly slice and add to the bowl. Mix by hand. Add the prawns and peanuts and mix through.

Now put the chillies in a mortar and crush them, followed by the garlic. Add the brown sugar, lime juice and fish sauce and mix through.

Add the sauce to the salad and mix everything together. Serve with a sprinkling of peanuts.

serves 4

prep 20 mins

cook 4 mins

rhubarb and sea bass

Rhubarb, to me, has always been savoury because my mum used to cook it with fish. I know now that it works both ways, but while I love a rhubarb pie or rhubarb jam, I still think it goes best with fish, so here I'm showing you my way of cooking rhubarb the way I always believed it should be. Cooked in garlic, with hints of turmeric and chilli, this is served with orzo and topped with a delicious slice of sea bass.

For the fish

2 tablespoons olive oil, plus extra to drizzle

4 sea bass fillets, skin on (400g)

¼ teaspoon ground turmeric

¼ teaspoon chilli powder

For the rhubarb orzo

3 cloves of garlic, minced

½ teaspoon ground turmeric

2 chillies, sliced lengthways

1 teaspoon salt

220g rhubarb, thinly sliced

300g orzo

700ml hot water

a handful of fresh coriander, chopped

2 tablespoons honey

Start by pouring the oil into a large, hot non-stick frying pan.

Put the sea bass fillets on a plate, sprinkle over the turmeric and chilli and mix to cover the entire fish.

Start cooking the fish skin-side down and, whatever you do, don't be tempted to move them. Cook for 4 minutes, then flip the fillets and cook for 1 minute more. Pop back onto the plate, cover and keep warm.

Pour some more oil into the pan, add the garlic and turmeric and cook for a few seconds. Add the chillies and rhubarb and cook for a few minutes till the rhubarb just begins to break down.

Add the orzo and stir through, then add the water and cook on high for about 10 minutes till the water has evaporated and the orzo is cooked. Take off the heat and stir through the coriander and honey.

Serve the orzo with a slice of the fish on top and a drizzling of oil.

serves 4　prep 15 mins　cook 20 mins

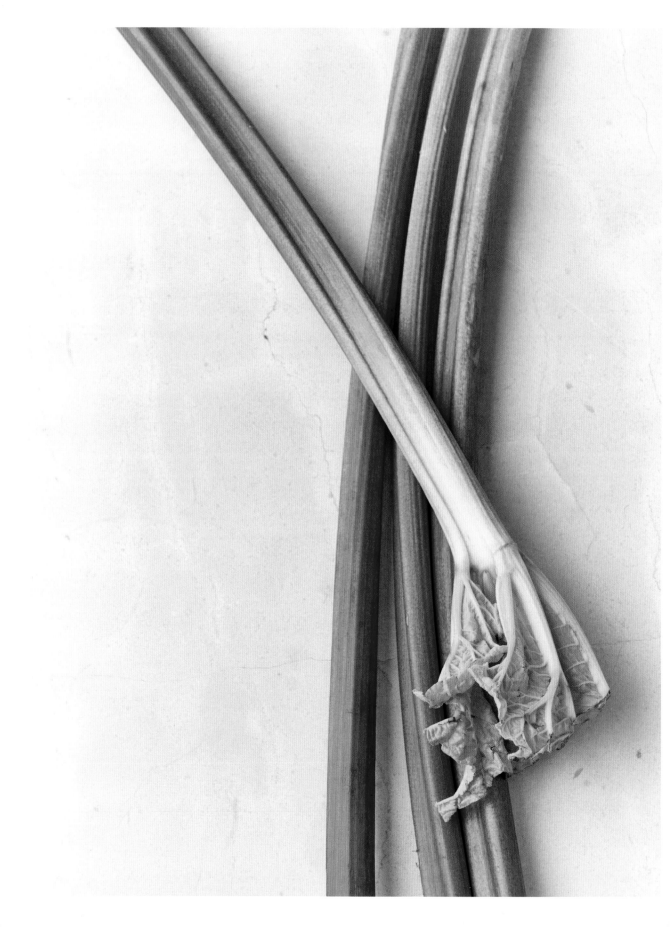

crabstick po boys

I first had a po boy out in Louisiana, a simple bread roll filled with deep-fried shrimp. Po boys are the kind of things I could eat for every meal of the day, for a very long time, and not get bored. My version is made with spiced crabsticks, packed with flavour and deep-fried into patties, piled into a buttered roll and drenched in a spicy-sweet, tangy apple sauce.

For the crabstick patties

250g crabsticks

1–2 green chillies, thinly sliced

2 red onions, thinly sliced

1 tablespoon coriander seeds, roughly crushed

1 tablespoon cumin seeds, roughly crushed

a small handful of fresh coriander, chopped

1 teaspoon salt

1 medium egg

70g chickpea flour

oil, for frying

For the apple sauce

200g chunky apple sauce

3 cloves of garlic, minced

4 tablespoons mayonnaise

½ lemon, juice only

a small handful of fresh coriander, chopped

To serve

4 submarine rolls

butter, for spreading

Start by making the patties. Scrape a fork along the length of the crabsticks to shred them. Pop into a bowl. Add the chilli, onion, coriander seeds, cumin seeds, coriander and salt. Mix with your hands.

Add the egg and chickpea flour and mix with your hands. If the mixture clumps when squeezed, it is ready.

Pop a frying pan on a high heat with 2–3cm of oil. Heat the oil to 180°C and as soon as the oil is hot, add clumps of the mixture, squeezing them to help bring the mixture together a little. Drop them into the oil, fry until dark golden brown and then flip over to cook the other side. Place on a plate with kitchen paper for the excess oil to drain. You will need to fry them in two batches and each batch will take about 4 minutes.

Now make the sauce by putting the apple sauce, garlic, mayo, lemon and coriander in a bowl and mixing together. Set aside.

Cut open the rolls lengthways down the side, butter the insides, smother over the apple sauce and fill with the hot patties.

serves 4   prep 25 mins   cook 15 mins

apple custard pie

I first made this by accident! One summer, leftover pastry in the fridge, too many apples from a windfall, a few egg yolks and a strong desire to bake (as usual!) and this thick, monumental pie was born. With its crumbly pastry, sweet/tart apple and smooth custard, the cold pie works well with a warm blackberry compote.

For the apple filling

10 eating apples (1.3kg), peeled, cored and sliced

55g caster sugar

40g unsalted butter

1 tablespoon cornflour

2 teaspoons ground cinnamon

For the pastry

265g plain flour

1½ tablespoons icing sugar

a pinch of salt

135g unsalted butter, cubed and cold

3–4 tablespoons cold water

for the custard

4 egg yolks

40g caster sugar

400ml double cream

1 teaspoon vanilla extract

1 teaspoon almond extract

For the blackberry compote

600g blackberries, halved

75g caster sugar

2 limes, juice and zest

Make the filling first so it has time to cool. Put the apples in a large saucepan along with the sugar, butter and cornflour and mix. Pop onto a medium heat and cook the apples down for 20 minutes with the lid on, making sure to stir occasionally. Take off the heat, add the cinnamon, mix and transfer to a flat plate to cool.

Now make the pastry. Put the flour in a food processor with the icing sugar and salt and whizz to combine. Add the butter and whizz till crumbly. Drizzle in the water and process till you have a mixture that just clumps together. Tip out and bring together without kneading. Shape into a flat disc and chill for 30 minutes.

Take a 20cm x 7cm deep round loose-bottomed cake tin. Roll out the pastry big enough to cover the base and sides with some overhang. I like to do this in between sheets of cling film to avoid using flour. Once the right size, pull off the top layer of cling film and flip the pastry into the cake tin. Peel off the other piece of cling film and shape the pastry around the base and sides of the tin. Once lined, cut off the overhang. Retain the cling film. Prick the base using a fork and pop into the freezer for 10 minutes.

Preheat the oven to 180°C/fan 160°C and pop a tray in.

Take the pastry out of the freezer and line with the cling film, making sure it hangs out over the side. Fill with baking beans or dry lentils, right to the top. Bake for 30 minutes on top of the hot tray. Remove from the oven, take out the cling film and baking beans, then bake again for 5–10 minutes until light golden and dry looking. Take out and set aside while you make the custard filling.

Put the egg yolks and sugar in a bowl and whisk. Add the cream, vanilla and almond extracts and mix.

Pour the apple filling into the pie case. Pour in the custard and coax it everywhere by gently stirring and moving the apples. Bake again for 1 hour–1 hour 10 minutes, till the centre has just set. Take out and leave to cool in the tin. Chill the pie overnight to set.

When you are ready to eat, make the compote. Add the blackberries to a pan. Use the back of a fork to squash a few to release the juices. Add the sugar, lime juice and zest and gently warm through on a medium heat. As soon as it begins to bubble, take it off the heat.

Serve a spoonful of warm compote with a chilled wedge of the pie. This is best eaten within a couple of days.

serves
10

prep
40 mins
+ setting

cook
40
mins

banana skin bagels

During lockdown I revealed my love of banana skins – nothing new to me, but new for many on social media. Yes, that banana peel that we all normally just throw away is edible and full of potassium. One of my favourite ways to cook it is simply in this garlicky barbecue sauce and wedged inside a chewy bagel with spicy cheese and pickle.

6 ripe bananas skins (about 400g)

4 tablespoons oil

2 small onions, thinly sliced

1 clove of garlic, minced

½ teaspoon salt

2 tablespoons barbecue sauce

2 tablespoons brown sauce

1 tablespoon ketchup

To serve

4 bagels

4 slices of spicy Mexican cheese

mayonnaise

8 slices of pickle

Wash the banana skins thoroughly and pat dry. Remove and discard the tough stalks, then chop the rest into thin strips about 3cm long.

Pour the oil into a small non-stick pan and turn the heat to medium. Add the onion and cook till golden brown and dark – this should take about 5–10 minutes, so not very long.

Add the garlic and stir through, cooking for a minute. Now add the banana skin and the salt and cook for 5 minutes. Add the barbecue sauce, brown sauce and the ketchup and mix through to warm.

Turn on the grill.

Take the bagels, slice in half and pop the eight slices on a tray. Cover the four bottom halves of the bagels with the banana skin mix. Add the cheese on top and grill everything till the cheese has really melted and the top halves are toasted golden.

Take out and add mayo to the four top halves. Add the pickles to the cheese, cover with the bagel tops and they are ready to devour.

recipe photographs over page ▶

serves 4

prep 15 mins

cook 15 mins

blueberry ice cream cake

Now you can have your cake and ice cream, and eat it too! There is no better way than when they are mooshed together. And I forgot to mention, there's biscuit here too: a coating of crunchy biscuit crumbs around soft Genoise sponge, quick blueberry ice cream and another layer of cake.

For the cake

4 medium eggs

125g caster sugar

100g unsalted butter, melted and cooled, plus extra for greasing

100g plain flour, sifted

For the ice cream

600ml double cream

170g condensed milk

1 tablespoon vanilla bean paste

200g blueberries

1 orange, zest only

3 tablespoons icing sugar, sifted (optional)

For the biscuit crumbs

50g chocolate digestives

2 teaspoons whole fennel seeds

Start by making the cake. Preheat the oven to 180°C/fan 160°C. Grease and line the base of a 20cm x 8cm deep round loose-bottomed cake tin.

Put the eggs and the sugar in a mixing bowl and whisk till the mixture is light and fluffy, so that when the whisk is lifted the mixture leaves a visible trail. This can take about 8 minutes.

Now add the melted butter around the edge of the egg mixture and whisk for a few seconds.

Add the flour and fold through till there are no floury lumps. Pour into the prepared tin and bake for 35 minutes until golden on top and slightly shrunk around the edges.

Once the cake is baked, leave in the tin for 10 minutes before removing to cool on a rack. Peel off the paper.

Wash the same tin, as we need to use the same one to assemble the cake. Grease and line the tin's base and sides and grease the paper on top too.

method continued over page ▶

serves 10

prep 40 mins + freezing

cook 40 mins

Add the fennel seeds to a small pan and toast very gently till golden brown and the oils are released from the seeds. Take off the heat.

Crumble the biscuits and the toasted fennel seeds to a fine crumb in a food processor (or bash in a food bag with the end of a rolling pin).

Make the ice cream by putting the cream in a bowl with the condensed milk and vanilla. Whip till just thick – this will take 5–10 minutes, then fold in the blueberries and orange zest.

Take the cake and cut in half horizontally so you have two rounds.

Take the tin out of the freezer. Lay the first layer of cake into the base. Take your biscuit and fennel crumbs and gently press onto the inside walls of the tin, covering all the way around, till you have used all the crumbs. Add the cream mixture on top.

Add the second layer of cake, cover the top to prevent freezer burn and leave in the freezer overnight or for at least 6 hours.

Remove the cake from the freezer 20 minutes before you plan to serve so that it will easily slice. The cake will keep in the freezer for up to 3 days. It is best eaten as soon as possible because it's a no-churn ice cream and will develop an 'icy' texture after a few days.

Enjoy! I know I will!

berry meringue roll

As meringues go, this is such a fun, roly-poly way of eating one, made with simple French meringue spread out into a tin with a layer of pistachios, before being baked and rolled up with lashings of cream, yoghurt, lime curd and raspberries. It's fresh, light and gets more and more delicious as it sits in the fridge – not that it will.

For the meringue
50g pistachios, roughly chopped

5 egg whites

275g caster sugar

For the filling
150ml double cream

150ml strawberry yoghurt

2 tablespoons lime curd

100g raspberries, halved

To serve
icing sugar, for dusting

Start by preheating the oven to 200°C/fan 180°C. Line a 33 x 23cm swiss roll tin. Sprinkle the chopped pistachios over the base.

Put the egg whites in a mixing bowl. Begin whipping and as soon as the mixture becomes frothy, start adding a spoonful of sugar, one spoon at a time, making sure the spoonful is incorporated each time. Once you have used up all the sugar, you should have a meringue that stands in stiff peaks and is glossy.

Take the mixture and spread into the tin, all over the chopped nuts. Make sure the top is even. Bake for 8 minutes. After 8 minutes, lower the temperature to 160°C/fan 140°C and bake for another 15 minutes.

Take the meringue, still in its paper, out of the tin and leave to cool completely. It will sink a bit as it sits.

Make the filling by whipping up the cream. As soon as the cream has thickened, mix through the yoghurt and then ripple through the lime curd.

Spread the mixture all over the meringue in an even layer. Dot over the raspberries, then roll the meringue up from the shorter end.

Pop onto a serving plate, seam-side down. Dust with icing sugar and leave in the fridge until ready to serve. Will keep in the fridge for up to 2 days.

serves
8

prep
20 mins
+ cooling

cook
25
mins

fruity

peach frangipane slices

These are delicious squares of sugar-glazed puff pastry, filled with a dense, cakey, almond filling and topped with soft sliced peaches. Sometimes, throwing pastry, cake and fruit together into a single dessert is exactly what you and I and everyone else needs!

375g ready-rolled puff pastry

100g unsalted butter, softened

100g caster sugar

2 medium eggs, plus 1 egg yolk

140g ground almonds

75g plain flour

1 teaspoon almond extract

4 small peaches, stones removed and each half thinly sliced and kept intact

sugar nibs, for sprinkling

1 tablespoon golden syrup, for glazing

Start by preheating the oven to 200°C/fan 180°C. Pop a baking tray in the oven. Line another tray with some baking paper.

Unroll the pastry and cut into quarters, so you have four rectangles. Put the pastry pieces onto the lined tray. Using the tip of a knife, score the inner edge of one of the quarters, 1cm in but not going all the way through. Pierce the inner rectangle all over. Do this to all four and pop into the fridge while you make the filling.

Place the butter and sugar in a bowl and mix till light and creamy. Break in the eggs and mix well. Add the almonds, flour and almond extract and mix till you have a thick batter.

Take the pastry out of the fridge and divide the batter among the four pastry sheets, spreading all the way to the edge of the scored border. This is a thick layer of filling about 1.5 – 2cm deep. Try to keep it within the lines of the border to minimize overspill when baking.

Add the peach slices, fanning out in one direction with one half and then fanning out the other half right next to it in the other direction.

Brush the edges with the egg yolk and sprinkle the edges with sugar nibs.

Put the lined tray on top of the preheated tray. Bake in the oven for 25 minutes until the pastry is risen and golden, and the frangipane is golden and firm to the touch. Take out and leave to cool on the tray until just slightly warm.

Glaze the fruit with the golden syrup and these are ready to eat. They will keep in the fridge for up to 2 days.

serves 4

prep 35 mins

cook 25 mins

SWEET

---

sweet shakshuka

Shakshuka is all the rage lately, it seems like everyone's making it. Perhaps because it's simple and easy and, let's face it, photographs beautifully. This is my sweet version made with lots of different fruits cooked in marmalade. And instead of eggs, the holes are filled with a cheesecake-like mixture and cooked gently. Sweet shakshuka!

For the fruit

2 tablespoons unsalted butter

400g plums, stones removed and quartered

300g strawberries, hulled and halved

150g blueberries

½ teaspoon ground cinnamon

3 tablespoons marmalade, with shreds

For the filling

250g ricotta

3 tablespoons plain flour

2 medium eggs

1 teaspoon vanilla bean paste

To serve

50g pistachios, roughly chopped

2 passion fruits, pulp removed

Start with a shallow casserole dish and pop onto a medium heat. Put in the butter and allow to melt. As soon as it's melted, add the plums and start cooking through till just starting to soften.

Add the strawberries, blueberries, cinnamon and marmalade, and mix through until the marmalade has dissolved. Lower the heat completely.

Make the filling by putting the ricotta, flour, eggs and vanilla paste in a bowl and mixing well.

Gently create four large dips in the fruit, then spoon the ricotta mixture into the spaces.

Pop the lid on the dish and leave the cheesecake mixture to steam for 12–15 minutes on a low heat.

As soon as it is cooked, take off the heat and sprinkle over the pistachios and passion fruit pulp.

serves 4

prep 15 mins

cook 30 mins

date and cardamom breakfast

Rice pudding is a staple in Bangladesh. It's often made with ground rice, but I find I miss the texture of actual grains of rice, so have made my version on a stove top using pudding rice. Not quite a risotto, not really a paella, but a sweet take on the same sort of idea, the rice cooked with milk and infused with cardamom. I serve it topped with a drizzling of sweet date coffee sauce and segments of orange.

For the rice

40g ghee

6 cardamom pods, crushed and seeds powdered

100g paella or pudding rice

350ml whole milk

80g caster sugar

For the sauce

150g dates, stoned

300ml boiling water

a pinch of salt

2 teaspoons instant coffee

2 oranges, segmented (reserve the zest)

Pop a small casserole dish on a medium heat on the hob. Put in the ghee and allow it to melt, then add the cardamom seeds and toast for a few seconds.

Add the rice and toast till the rice is just lightly golden.

Add the milk and sugar and stir, then bring the mixture to a boil. Reduce the heat completely and leave covered, on a low heat on the smallest ring, for 40 minutes to an hour, until the rice is cooked and the milk has thickened.

Make the sauce by putting the dates in a bowl with the boiling water. Add the salt, coffee and the zest of the oranges. Once the water is warm and the dates have softened, blitz to a smooth paste in a food processor.

Take the pudding off the heat, drizzle over the date sauce and add the orange segments to finish.

serves 4   prep 10 mins   cook 1 hour

duck tostadas

Tostadas are one of my family's go-to things to eat, snack on and enjoy, but finding large tostada-style crisps can be hard, so we make our own using tortilla wraps fried till they're crisp. Here they're topped with hoisin and duck that's been cooked in sweet cola and lime till it's sticky and coated. This recipe takes inspiration from several parts of the world – when I can't decide where to go, I go everywhere!

For the duck

330ml cola

½ teaspoon ground cinnamon

1 lime, zest and juice

1 teaspoon salt

2 teaspoons ginger paste

1 teaspoon chilli paste

2 tablespoons ketchup

340g duck breast, skin removed, sliced into strips

1 tablespoon cornflour

oil, for frying

1 red pepper, sliced

1 yellow pepper, sliced

4 large tortilla wraps

To serve

hoisin sauce

½ cucumber, peeled and thinly sliced

3 spring onions, thinly sliced

2 chillies, thinly sliced

a sprinkling of sesame seeds

Start by putting the cola, cinnamon, lime zest and juice, salt, ginger, chilli and ketchup in a small saucepan and mixing together. Put onto a medium heat and heat until boiling, then cook until reduced to about half and really thickened.

Dust the duck breast in the cornflour till just coated. Pour a small drizzle of oil into a pan and heat. Add the duck breast and cook till browned, then add the peppers and cook till just soft. Add the reduced sauce and mix through, then cook until the duck and peppers are coated.

Pour a thin layer of oil into a frying pan. Add some kitchen paper to a plate. Fry the tortillas till they are crisp and golden on both sides. Drain on the paper.

To serve, spread each crisp tortilla with some hoisin sauce, add the duck mixture, cucumber, spring onion, chilli and sesame seeds and you are ready to eat.

serves
4

prep
10 mins

cook
15–20 mins

honey-baked sriracha drumsticks

Drumsticks are another go-to in our house; we think they're the best bit of the chicken. These are coated in garlic, sriracha sauce and plenty of honey to make them sticky, and roasted till the skin is crispy. This is the perfect recipe not only for indoors but also for the barbecue, especially when served with a delicious potato salad. The drumsticks are also delicious served with the coronation aubergine on page 172.

For the drumsticks

10 drumsticks (700g), skin on

3 tablespoons oil, plus extra for greasing the tray

3 cloves of garlic, minced

4 tablespoons soy sauce

4 tablespoons sriracha sauce

3 tablespoons runny honey

½ teaspoon ground star anise

2 tablespoons cornflour

For the potato salad

567g tin of new potatoes, halved

1 carrot, peeled and grated

6 tablespoons mayo

2 pickled eggs, grated

1 heaped tablespoon wholegrain mustard

1 tablespoon honey

a large handful of chopped fresh chives

a good pinch of salt

chopped fresh coriander, to serve

Start by making the chicken. Put the drumsticks in a large pan and pour water over the top till they are submerged. Pop onto the heat and bring up to the boil, leave to simmer for 5 minutes and then drain. Set aside.

Preheat the oven to 200°C/fan 180°C. Grease a baking tray lightly with oil.

Put the oil, garlic, soy, sriracha, honey, star anise and cornflour in a large bowl and mix well. Pat the chicken pieces dry and mix into the sauce. Lay onto the tray in an even layer and bake for 30 minutes, making sure to turn halfway through.

Make the salad by putting the drained potatoes in a bowl with the grated carrot and mixing together. In a smaller bowl, mix together the mayo, grated egg, wholegrain mustard and honey. Pour the dressing into the potato bowl and mix till coated. Add the chives and salt and mix.

Once ready, sprinkle the chicken with chopped coriander, if you like, and it is ready to serve with the potato salad.

serves 5   prep 15 mins   cook 30–35 mins

stem ginger beef

Stem ginger is often just used in sweet baking but it works really well in savoury too, especially with beef. Cooked simply with a few spices, the sweetness of the ginger really shines. This is served with a buttery, oat-infused skirlie mash.

for the beef

4 tablespoons oil

7–8cm ginger, peeled and cut into matchsticks, plus extra to serve

450g beef (shin or brisket would work well), thinly sliced

1 tablespoon ground cumin

1 tablespoon ground black pepper

2 onions, thinly sliced

1 teaspoon salt

2 tablespoons tamarind

2 rounds of stem ginger, grated

300ml water

chopped fresh parsley, to garnish

For the skirlie mash

1kg potatoes, peeled and quartered

100g butter

2 onions, diced

50g oats

200ml cream

a big pinch of salt

5 tablespoons mayonnaise

Start by making the beef. Pour the oil into a large frying pan and when the oil is hot, add the ginger and cook for few minutes. Add the beef and cook till brown. Add the cumin and pepper and heat through, then add the onion and salt and mix. Cook till soft.

Add the tamarind, stem ginger and water. Bring to the boil and leave to simmer while you make the mash.

To make the mash, boil the potatoes until soft, and then drain. Pop back into the pan.

Put the butter in a medium frying pan and melt. Add the onion and cook till brown, adding the oats halfway through to cook.

Mash the potatoes, add the cream and onion, then mix together. Add the salt and mayo and mix again.

Serve the skirlie mash with the beef, with the parsley sprinkled over the top.

serves 4   prep 10 mins   cook 35 mins

sweet potato Eccles cake

Eccles cakes are dangerously good, to the point where I can eat and not really know when to stop. This is a giant savoury version, made like the easiest, simplest pie, with shop-bought puff pastry. It is filled with sweet potatoes and salty feta cheese, then topped with pine nuts, baked and cut into wedges. Why have small Eccles cakes when you can have one that looks like it was made for the BFG!?

500g block of puff pastry

flour, for dusting

1 egg, beaten

Parmesan cheese, finely grated

For the filling

2 sweet potatoes

100g feta

a few leaves of fresh basil

3 tablespoons green pesto

50g pine nuts

Start by making the filling. Bake the sweet potatoes in the oven or microwave till the flesh inside is soft. Scoop out the flesh into a bowl and leave to cool.

Mash up the cooled flesh and crumble in the feta. Tear in the basil. Add the pesto and pine nuts and mix through. Set aside.

Take the puff pastry and knead quickly to break up the even lamination and create a rougher layer texture. Dust the surface with some flour and roll the dough out until you have a circle that is about 30cm across. Add the filling and spread to about a 23cm round.

Bring the edges in to create a sealed circle, making sure to pinch the pastry together. Using a cake lifter or baking tray, lift off the surface and flip the sealed side down onto a baking tray.

Pop into the fridge for 30 minutes to an hour.

Preheat the oven to 160°C/fan 140°C.

Take the Eccles cake out, glaze all over with the egg wash and sprinkle over the cheese. Make three slits in the top, each about 4cm long. Bake for 40–45 minutes. If after about 25 minutes the cake begins to colour too much, cover with foil.

Take out, leave to just cool and it's ready to eat, cut into wedges.

serves 5

prep 15 mins + chilling

cook 45 mins

baked beans dirty rice

Dirty rice, in our house, is basically anything and everything mixed with rice. But putting 'anything and everything' on an ingredients list just doesn't cut it in a recipe book, so I've written one up for you, using one of my favourite sweet-savoury ingredients, a good old tin of baked beans.

10 tablespoons oil

4 large cloves of garlic, thinly sliced

2 teaspoons fennel seeds, lightly crushed

2 red onions, diced

1 red pepper, diced

2 teaspoons salt

1 tablespoon paprika

340g tin of corned beef, mashed

410g tin of baked beans

400g basmati rice

800ml hot water

100g frozen peas

To serve

lemon wedges

crispy fried onions

chillies

chopped fresh coriander

eggs

chilli oil

Start by pouring the oil into a large non-stick pan with a tight-fitting lid. Place on a high heat. As soon as the oil is hot, add the garlic and cook until golden brown. As soon as it is, add the fennel seeds and mix. Now add the onion and cook till they too are very golden in colour.

Add the pepper and cook till just soft. Add the salt and paprika, mix in and cook for a minute.

Add the corned beef and beans and mix well. Add the rice and cook on a high heat for 3 minutes.

Pour in the hot water and mix on a high heat till you can see the rice grains and the liquid has thickened. Add the peas, mix and pop the lid on, reducing the heat to the lowest setting. Leave to steam for 10 minutes.

As soon as the rice is cooked, take the lid off and leave for 10 minutes before serving.

Serve with your choice of a lemon wedge, crispy onions, chilli, coriander, eggs and/or chilli oil.

serves 4 · prep 15 mins · cook 40 mins

Anzac pudding

Anzac is my Abdal's all-time favourite biscuit, so you can imagine his delight to eat his favourite biscuit in pudding form. This has all the familiar flavours of Anzac with its oats and coconut, plus a layer of fruit cocktail and white chocolate on the base.

70g oats

170g desiccated coconut

200g plain flour

170g light brown sugar

200g butter

3 tablespoons golden syrup

1 teaspoon bicarbonate of soda

2 x 411g tins of fruit cocktail, drained

100g white chocolate, finely chopped

custard or ice cream, to serve

Start by putting the oats, coconut and plain flour in a bowl and mixing. Take a large non-stick pan, pop onto a medium heat and dry fry the oats mix till golden. You will have to do this in two, maybe three, batches to ensure an even colour. As soon as it is golden, transfer to a bowl.

Put the sugar and butter in a small pan with the golden syrup and heat till the sugar has melted. Take off the heat and add the bicarbonate of soda. Add the sugar mix into the dry oat mix and stir through.

Preheat the oven to 170°C/fan 150°C.

Put the drained fruit cocktail in a 23 x 33cm casserole dish. Sprinkle the chopped white chocolate all over the top. Add the Anzac mixture on top of the fruit and bake for 15–20 minutes.

Take out and leave for 10 minutes for the Anzac to crisp up. Serve with hot custard or cold ice cream or both.

serves
6

prep
15 mins

cook
25 mins

coffee-glazed focaccia

Of all the breads, focaccia is one of my faves. Okay, all bread is my fave, but focaccia is in my top five. The texture is chewy and light, and it's always full of flavour, especially when doused in good oil. Well, here I made my own version, sweet and coffee-laden. The dough is rippled with walnuts, brushed with sweet coffee oil, baked and drizzled with a coffee glaze. If we are going to bend the rules, we may as well get close to breaking point.

500g strong bread flour

7g fast-action yeast

2 teaspoons sugar

1 teaspoon salt

380ml warm water

50g walnuts, roughly chopped

1 tablespoon hot water

1 teaspoon instant coffee

3 tablespoons oil, plus extra for greasing

For the coffee glaze

200g icing sugar

2 tablespoons hot water

2 teaspoons instant coffee

Start by putting the flour and yeast in a bowl with the sugar and salt and mixing. Make a well in the centre. Add the warm water and mix till you bring the dough together.

If you are kneading by hand, knead on a lightly floured surface till the dough is smooth and stretchy. Alternatively attach a dough hook to a freestanding mixer and knead on high for 10 minutes. Take the dough out and leave in a greased bowl to rise till double in size.

When risen, take the dough out and whack all the air out. Sprinkle over the chopped nuts and knead in.

Lightly grease a 25 x 35cm tin or tray. Add the dough and spread the dough into the tin using your fingers to create dimples. It helps to lightly oil your hands to stretch the dough. Cover with greased cling film and leave to rise for 20 minutes in a warm place till the tray looks like it's been filled.

Preheat the oven to 200°C/fan 180°C.

Remove the cling film from the dough. Using fingers, dimple the dough all over.

Put the hot water in a bowl with the coffee, stir to dissolve, then add the oil and mix. Drizzle all over the dough and bake for 20 minutes.

Make the glaze by putting the icing sugar in a bowl. Add the hot water with the coffee and mix.

As soon as the focaccia comes out of the oven, brush over the icing and it is ready to chop and chomp!

serves 6

prep 1 hour 20 mins

cook 20–25 mins

doughnut lamb burgers

This is one of those recipes that makes you think, 'I couldn't!', when really you could, and even if you think you can't, you actually can – and I know you want to! The lamb mince is simply seasoned and flavoured and mixed with cheese, then shaped into patties and griddled, ready to be topped with crisp bacon and jalapeños, and all sandwiched inside a grilled sugar doughnut.

For the lamb patties

400g lamb mince

1 teaspoon salt

1 teaspoon ground black pepper

1 tablespoon onion granules

1 tablespoon garlic granules

2 tablespoons plain flour

1 medium egg

50g Cheddar cheese, finely grated

oil, for frying

To serve

4 glazed ring doughnuts, halved

8 rashers of crispy bacon

jalapeños

To make the patties, put the mince in a bowl. Add the salt, pepper, onion, garlic and plain flour and mix through. Add the egg and cheese and mix till the cheese is well combined.

Divide into four equal patties, 1cm thick. Brush each patty with some oil.

Lightly grease a griddle pan and put on a medium heat. Cook each patty for 3 minutes on each side. Take the patties off and pop on a plate.

Griddle the halved doughnuts, glazed-side down, in the same pan to caramelize the sugar.

Add the patties to one half of the doughnuts, top with the bacon, jalapeños and the other doughnut halves and they're ready to eat.

serves 4

prep 10 mins

cook 10–15 mins

malva cakes

I discovered this cake on my travels to South Africa. It is sweet and sticky and if I was going to compare it to anything, I would say it's the South African version of a sticky toffee pudding. This recipe is for individual cakes, baked with chewy apricots and then doused in a hot apricot jam sauce. It is the kind of sweet that sticks to the roof of your mouth, which to me is the best kind.

For the cakes

oil, for greasing

30g roasted chopped hazelnuts

150g unsalted butter, softened

150g soft brown sugar

3 medium eggs

150g self-raising four, sifted

a pinch of salt

75g dried apricots, chopped

For the sauce

50g unsalted butter

50g apricot jam

100ml single cream

ice cream, to serve (optional)

Preheat the oven to 180°C/fan 160°C. Grease the holes of a 12-hole deep muffin tin. Inside the base of each one, sprinkle in the chopped hazelnuts. Set aside.

Make the batter by putting the butter and sugar in a bowl and whisk till light and creamy. Add one egg at a time till combined. Add the flour and the salt and mix till you have a smooth batter. Stir in the dried apricots.

Divide the mix into the holes and bake for 20–22 minutes.

While they bake, make the sauce. Put the butter and jam in a small saucepan and cook till the mixture is golden and even. Add the cream and whisk while bringing to the boil. Simmer for a few minutes till you have an even mixture.

As soon as the cakes are out of the oven, make holes all over them using a skewer, making sure to go all the way down to the base. Pour over the hot sauce and leave till the cakes are just cooled, then carefully remove and serve. If you like, you can top each one with ice cream.

makes 12

prep 10 mins

cook 20–22 mins

red velvet cake

This is my boy's all-time favourite cake. With its two layers of bold, red, cocoa-flavoured sponge and hints of almond and vanilla, sandwiched and covered with rich vanilla cream-cheese frosting and simply but beautifully decorated, you can see why it's his favourite.

For the cake

250g unsalted butter, softened, plus extra for greasing the tins

300g caster sugar

3 medium eggs

50g cocoa powder

1 teaspoon red gel food colouring

1 teaspoon vanilla extract

1 teaspoon almond extract

300g plain flour, sifted

240ml buttermilk

1 tablespoon white vinegar

1 teaspoon bicarbonate of soda

For the cream cheese icing

100g unsalted butter, softened

600g icing sugar, sifted

250g full-fat cream cheese

1 teaspoon vanilla bean extract

Preheat the oven to 160°C/fan 140°C. Grease and line 2 x 20cm cake tins.

Start by putting the butter and sugar into a bowl and whisking till light and fluffy. Add the eggs in one by one till combined. Add the cocoa, food colouring, vanilla and almond extracts and mix till combined.

Add half the flour and half the buttermilk and mix through. Do the same again and add the rest of the flour and then the rest of the buttermilk.

When you have a smooth batter, mix the vinegar with the bicarb, then add to the batter. Mix into a smooth batter and divide between the two tins, level off and bake for 40 minutes.

Take out and leave to cool in the tin for 10 minutes and then on a cooling rack.

Make the icing by whipping together the butter and icing sugar. Add the cream cheese and vanilla and mix in.

As soon as the cakes are cooled, level off the tops and save the crumbs. Sandwich the cake layers with the icing and cover the top and sides. Crumble up the scraps and cover the base of the sides.

recipe photographs over page ▶

serves
8

prep
20
mins

cook
40
mins

thanks

It takes a village to put a book together, I kid you not! Not a word of exaggeration when I think about the amount of time and the many people it takes to get us to the stage where we have a gorgeous polished book that sits on shelves in people's homes, on tables, bookmarked, pages folded, ready to create something delicious.

Thank you to the recipe testers, Katy Gilhooly and Georgia May, for going through the recipes to make sure they all work as they should, the job I would be doing if I were not doing this!

Thank you, Chris Terry, for the forever beautiful photography: just when we think we have got the shot he does another one, and then we think we've got the shot, and then it turns out we like the first one anyway!

Thank you, Rob Allison and Hollie Cochrane, for doing recipe after recipe, dish after dish, and not hating me afterwards! But Hollie, mostly thank you for the best croissants I have ever tasted in my entire life.

Thank you, Roya Fraser, for bringing with you your style, your detail and all the props in the world, and I will always enjoy our mutual love for Russian Blues!

Thank you, Georgia Glynn Smith of N5 Studios: I come as much for the studio as I do for your beautiful doggo!

Thank you, Sarah Fraser, for always putting together something new and beautiful, each and every time! Your vision always takes my breath away, page after page after page.

Anne Kibel and Heather Marnie, thank you, chief taste-tester extraordinaires!

Thank you, Ione Walder, for always just being there, except for when you're on leave, but that doesn't matter because I have your number, so there is no escaping me! Thank you for always supporting me.

Thank you, Dan Bunyard, we can count on you to turn up at midday when lunch and all the food in the world is served up! 'This doesn't need photographing, does it?' Thank you for believing in me.

Thank you to the entire team – Laura Nicol, Bea McIntyre, Beth O'Rafferty, Dan Prescott-Bennett, Gail Jones, Claire Collins, Emma Plater, Ella Watkins, Sophie Shaw, Anjali Nathani, Vanessa Forbes, Liz Smith and everyone else behind the scenes – for being a part of our little village! We did it again!

Thank you, Abdal, Musa, Dawud and Maryam for simply eating what I cook. Do I care for your opinion? Absolutely not, it's food and it tastes good, so eat!

Home is a big sentiment, it can mean many things, but thank you, Michael Joseph, for helping me find a little bit of home with you!

index

michael joseph

UK | USA | Canada | Ireland | Australia
India | New Zealand | South Africa

Michael Joseph is part of the Penguin
Random House group of companies
whose addresses can be found at
global.penguinrandomhouse.com.

First published in Great Britain by
Michael Joseph, 2021
001

By arrangement with the BBC
BBC Logo copyright © BBC, 1996
The BBC logo is a registered trademark
of the British Broadcasting Corporation
and is used under licence

TV series produced by Wall to Wall Media Ltd

wall to wall
A WARNER BROS. TELEVISION
PRODUCTION UK COMPANY

Set in Bauer Grotesk OT

Colour reproduction by Altaimage Ltd
Printed in Italy by Printer Trento Ltd S.r.L.

A CIP catalogue record for this book is
available from the British Library

ISBN: 978-0-241-45322-3

www.greenpenguin.co.uk